The Art and Craft of Cover Design

A Comprehensive
Book Cover Design Guide
for the Self-Publisher

Gene Stirm

Although the author and publisher have made every effort to ensure that the information in this book was correct at press time, the author and publisher do not assume and hereby disclaim any liability to any party for any loss, damage, or disruption caused by errors or omissions, whether such errors or omissions result from negligence, accident, or any other cause.

The information in this book was written and published as a reference for those interested in or involved in cover design, choosing a book cover or self-publishing. It is not meant to replace professional legal or financial advice and comes with no guarantees of success.

The printing, POD and publishing industry along with the Internet are in a constant state of flux, we therefore cannot guarantee the information and resources herein will always be current. It is our intention to offer you the most updated information available and give you the tools and information to locate the additional resources you need.

 Printed in the United States of America. For information address: Way West Production, 1220 Alder Ave. Tehachapi, California, 93561.

ISBN-13: 978-0-9826828-1-4

First Edition
First printing, September 2010

Photoshop, Photoshop LE, Acrobat and Adobe are registered trademarks of Adobe Systems Incorporated.

About the Author

Gene Stirm fell in love with the arts at an early age. In high school he was active in art and theater. Winning honors in display design and stage design, including the Bank of America Award for Fine Art. He established himself as an artist, actor, director, and set designer, so after high school he gathered his friends together and started his own local theater production company in Santa Clara, California.

After two years of college and a number of personal and family conflicts, he chose to move to the mountains. Taking a year to try to find himself, he figured he wasn't really lost, and focused his direction towards commercial art and graphic design. He had already spent several years as an ER Technician, sign painter and restaurant owner. Finishing art school in 1971, he went to work for a weekly newspaper and commercial printing company in Central California. With the knowledge of printing now reinforcing his graphic art and design skills, he took a position as a studio artist at a full-service advertising agency. There, he participated in everything from typesetting, illustrations and photography to storyboarding, copywriting and even direct commercials for TV. Within a year with the advertising agency, he was hired as art director for Josten's American Yearbook Company, in Visalia, California where he continued studying book design and photography including study with Ansel Adams, even guest lectured at the Ansel Adams Workshops in Yosemite.

Moving to Orange County, California, and after managing two printing companies, doors opened in the area of menu design where he combined his restaurateur knowledge with his art training and cover design experience. His work was in demand and he and a partner started Stirm/Collins & Associates, a menu design company with a client list that included, The Fairmont Corporation, The Plaza NY, The Beverly Wilshire, The Bel Air and Halekulani. Along the way, he filled his spare time by teaching painting, floral design and photography, along with painted murals, designed sets for professional production in LA and Orange County, and raised orchids.

Upon selling the menu business, he returned to acting, and dabbled in filmmaking and screen writing with a special interest in documentary. His first documentary effort won a VIC award in 2001 and 2002 he wrote and produced the feature film, Birthday Wishes.

In 2004, he and his wife moved to Tehachapi, California, where he continued his studies of Native American art and culture and Shamanism. It was at that time he began rewriting a number of his screenplays into novels. In 2008, he received a Doctor of Shamanism Degree from ULC Seminary.

Gene has been connected with publishing, book design and editing most of his professional life. Writing credits include: Editor of Impression, Josten's employee magazine; writer and editor, OC Orchid Society Bulletin; a photographic book, *O Israel, Is Your Fig Tree Budding* and the novel; *Mystical Path To Mystique*, is his first novel published 2010.

To my girls,
Patricia,
Malinda and Bethany

Acknowledgment

To acknowledge everyone in a work of this sort is impossible. It comes from forty years of adventure in the graphic art business and the hundred of associates, co-worker and clients I have had along the way. I am humbly grateful to all those who shared their knowledge, pushed me to excellence and maintained faith in me. I offer an indebted thank you. And no one deserves greater acknowledgment than my loving wife Patricia.

Table of Contents

PART TWO

INTRODUCTION

If a dyslexic kid from Hood River, Oregon, can learn to design covers that sell for thousands of dollars, anyone can master the basics of good cover design.

While it's true, you can't judge a book by its cover, one often buys a book because of it's cover, if that were not so, mainline publishers wouldn't be spending millions of dollars each year on cover designs. I've worked for more than forty years in the graphic arts, cover design and printing industry. As a professional designer, I can assure you, *covers do sell books.*

For the self-publisher, a good, eye-catching cover is your first marketing tool. Even the postage size black and white imaged viewed on a Kindle, speaks volumes about the book for sale. A well designed cover will stand-out, and when you are competing with the BIG BOYS of publishing on an almost level playing field that Amazon offers the self-publisher, covers do count.

This book, while written for the novice, is full of information, innovation and tricks-of-the-trade that come from years of experience in the business and will help anyone involved in self-publishing, designing or choosing a cover for a book.

I want to thank my colleagues and new friends that are writing how to books for Kindle, CreateSpace or POD providers and especially on topics of self-publishing and book layout. This book will complement their noble efforts. Digital publishing and print on demand, POD, is as revolutionary as Gutenberg's invention of movable type, in opening an access to new material, ideas and thoughts without the very oppressive filter of mainline publishers.

THE ART AND CRAFT OF BOOK COVER DESIGN

Over the past 40 years, the craft of book covers and printing in general has change dramatically, especially in the area of prepress and prep, due to the development of desktop-publishing. The changes I have seen could fill a book in itself. We have just experienced the second greatest revolution in printing.

I finished art school with a degree in commercial art in 1971. It didn't take many job interviews to realize I had learned the art of graphic design, but not the craft. I apprenticed myself to a commercial printer that also published a weekly newspaper. I learned my craft quickly and in a little over a year; I was the Art Director at Josten's, American Yearbook Company in Visalia, California. The Visalia facility produced more than 2000 yearbooks and hundreds of commercial books yearly. All the cover art passed through my art department. At peak season, I had 45 artists working for me. I eventually left Josten's and opened my own print shop and later a menu design company that catered to the high-end hospitality industry.

In my initial concept for this book, I had intended to include step-by-step instructions, but with so many design programs available and POD providers now offering on-line cover design tools, the instructions would be obsolete before I could upload the text to the printer. This book will focus on the overall art and craft of cover design from the conceptualization of the front cover to effect use of the back cover as a marketing tool. The basics of cover designs for paperback and dust jackets for hardback books have changes little, but with the advent of desktop publishing, the craft of actual producing a cover is constantly changing. The freedom afforded the cover designer today opens new creative avenues and challenges. I have always believed tools without knowledge does not build much of a house or in this case, create an effective cover.

PART ONE

Chapter 1

ELEMENTS OF A BOOK COVER

Elements of a book's front cover can be broken down into four categories.

TYPOGRAPHY, GRAPHICS, (illustrations or photographs) COLOR and APPEAL Missing any one of these elements weaken the effectiveness of the cover. It is that simple.

TITLE TYPOGRAPHY

When I began working for the newspaper, one of my tasks was to write and set headlines. Think of your title as a headline for your book, the hook that entices a buyer. Let's face it; unless you're giving your books away free, if you don't have buyers, you don't have readers. Selling your books should be the motivation behind your title, as well as every aspect of self-publishing.

There, I did it; I snuck that dirty word SELL in on you. After investing your time in writing your book, you want to make it available to the reader. If you choose to self-publish, once your book is at the printer or the POD service, it is all about Marketing and Selling. If selling your book is not your goal, print out a dozen copies of your book on your home printer, bind them together and give them away. However, remember, for most people, a free book is worth what they paid for it, nothing. If you want to give your work away, that's your business. I believe a writer should be paid for their work. Your effort to write a book, edit, format and self-publish is worth something. So I repeat, the first step in marketing your book, is your cover. That means spending the time needed to create an effective cover, including learning how to do it yourself, or pay someone to do it for you.

Today typography is no big deal. In the past, you had to have the typeset by professional typesetters. Now with desktop publishing, you highlight a line of type and click on any of hundreds of type style and sizes. However, before I go any further with typestyles and sizes, you have to have copy. For a cover, the two key lines of type on your book's front cover are the title and author's name.

Let's start with the title. Most writers I know start with at least a working title before they start writing. It sets the stage for the book. Which comes first, the title or the book is like arguing the Chicken or the Egg. For me, I start with a working title that may change a dozen times. Some writers start writing without a title, but before you publish, it must have a title. There are two types of titles, allusive and descriptive. The allusive title is just that, a few words that convey a mood, theme or place. The allusive is usual used on works of fiction. *Angels and Demons, Murder on the Orient Express, It Happened in Reno,* are examples of allusive titles. Though they might give a hint of the story, such as murder, they keep their mystique. Don't use an allusive title on non-fiction if you want to sell your book.

The second form of titles is the descriptive. Descriptive titles tell the reader precisely what the book is about in the least possible words and are extensively used with non-fiction.

Aaron Shepard in his book *Aiming at Amazon*, points out the importance of a descriptive title to drive search engines to your book. When you are competing in the world's largest book market, take every legitimate advantage you can. Aaron says to use ever-available character in your title and subtitle description to help a potential buyer find your book. How long can your book's title be? Your listed title on Amazon can be up to 200 characters, including punctuation and spaces.

If you are going to self-publish on Amazon, the home of CreateSpace and the Kindle, I recommend Aaron Shepard's book, *Aiming at Amazon*. Aaron's book is available on amazon.com.

AUTHOR'S NAME

Yes, an author's name is the next element. Some are happy with their name, others aren't. If you have a long complicated name that might turn reader away, shorten it or choose a pen name. Sometimes our given name happens to be the same as some other famous writer, say Steven King, Mark Twain or Dan Brown. If yours is such, you should change or alter it. Nothing irritates a reader more than buying a Steven King novel to find it's by Steven King from Olancha, California, and not the famous author they were expecting. How you modify it is up to you. First initial middle name, two initials or a nickname, whatever you want, just make it different, and research it before you use it. Make sure nobody else is using the name. Do a search on the Internet.

Another reason for using a pen name is anonymity. Say you are a published writer, and you want to produce a work in another genre, and don't want your name connected with that genre, you might choose a pen name. Warning, eventually the names will be connected.

Ethnic names are often modified for prejudicial reasons, along with female names when writing in a mans market or vice versa. It's unfair, but there is a lot of prejudice out there in the market place. However, there are times when an unusual name may be to your advantage, then use your real name. Be careful with phony sounding names like Flash Writer, Hot Pen or Fast Hands, you want to sound credible at least.

My given name is Eugene, but I have gone by Gene all my life. However, when income is reported under Gene Stirm, instead of Eugene Stirm, it creates a mess with the IRS. So, be careful with tax forms. My name as Gene Stirm is registered with the Screen Actors Guild and no other member can use the same or similar name. The same holds true with Writer's Guild members, but if your not a Guild member, nothing prevents you from using any name you choose, unless that name's registered to a celebrity or their estate, names are not copyrighted, but can be registered trademarks. Don't try calling your book *Memoirs of a Cowboy, by Jack Palance.* His estate would be after you in a minute, even if your book had nothing to do with the late actor/writer Jack Palance, and if your name actually was Jack Palance. You might spend years in court fighting over something avoidable with a J. J. Palance or Jackson Palance.

Just as names cannot be copyrighted, titles are not copyrightable either, but might be registered or trademarked, visit www.copyright.gov. Every writer should know the basics of the copyright laws.

Lastly, do your research; you don't want your title or name lost in a sea of same or similar titles. Be willing to modify or change if needed.

ILLUSTRATIONS AND PHOTOGRAPH

As a professional illustrator and photographer, this is an area of prim interest to me. However, your graphic elements can be as simple as a border or a few blocks of color. If you're not a trained artist or photographer, buy what you need from a professional source. Photographs and illustrations from photo bank services are very inexpensive, as low as ten bucks. I have some sources listed at the back of this book.

If you have a picture or drawing by Uncle Frank that you are heart-set on having on your cover, get a second opinion, or even a third or fourth, and make sure it isn't Aunt Maple. Get the most professional opinion you can find and make sure they are unbiased. Not a photographer or artist saying it's lousy, so they can sell you theirs own work. But you don't want someone that agrees with you just because they don't want to hurt feelings either.

Second, make sure your graphics are appropriate to your subject. If your book is about growing potted plants, don't put a picture of a car on the cover, unless the car is a planter.

COLOR

With a rainbow as your pallet, the right color can sell books and the wrong color can destroy sales. Everyone is color prejudice, it's biological, a natural built in defense. Food colors for instance, meat is red, salads are green, if someone put a green steak on a plate, will you eat it? Green means go and red means stop, except in sex then red means go, but green lipstick just doesn't work. And for Kindle covers and newsprint, don't forget white, black, and shades of gray are colors.

More money is spent on color research then you can imagine, IBM's blue, Adobe's red and the *For Dummies* book series yellow, are colors that were agonized over for months before they were chosen. As a printer, I know that companies spent more time scrutinizing the color of their logo on a press-proof then they do anything else. Most company logos are printed in their company's own, specially mixed inks and if there was the slightest variance of color in the press run, the job is rejected. I'm not saying you have to be that picky, but color is important in sales and marketing.

APPEAL

Yes, for a cover to sell a book it must be appealing, and sex is the most appealing. That doesn't mean you have to have torrid, near pornographic photo on your cover, but it has to be appealing. Remember sex sells, *always*. If you really want an education in how effective sex is used in advertising, do a study into subliminal advertising, you will be shocked at how sex sells everything, including religion.

Typography, graphics, color and appeal, are the four elements that will make or break your cover. Book covers sell books, make your book cover sell your book.

Chapter 2

TYPOGRAPHY

As I stated earlier, typesetting has changed dramatically in the last couple of decades, and as desktop computers get more powerful the simplicity of setting your own type get even easier. In addition, you now have the tools to produce type with style and dynamics to fit your book cover's needs without being a trained typographer. There are simply a few basic rules to master and a couple of pitfalls to avoid.

Typefaces are the basis of all typography. When desktop publishing was in its infancy, Adobe Type Manager with Adobe fonts, were the only software that allowed quality type to be set and out-put to film from a desktop computers. From personal experience, I find that for cover creation using Photoshop, it is best to use only the Adobe typestyles that came with your software. If you use software other then Adobe's, I again encourage you to stay with the type fonts that come with your software unless you are confident in your computer skills and imbedding all the needed information when you create your PDF files for uploading your cover to your printer.

Front cover type, called display type, is usually, bigger, bolder and fancier than type that is used for the body of your book. When you set display type, you have virtually infinite variations to make it entirely your own art. To appreciate what your software can do, you have to play with it. Try out different typestyles. Print out samples and make notes. Remember, readability is the number one criteria of any typestyle.

FONTS

A font is an assortment of type, an alphabet plus numbers, punctuation marks and sometime symbols. Most fonts have both capitals and lower case, called uppercase and lowercase, a term carried over from the hand typesetting days. Not all fonts have both upper and lower case letters.

There are two families of fonts. Serf or Roman letters have embellishments at the beginning and ending of the stroke. The embellishment was originally from the starting and end of the chisel when letters were carved in stone. The other font family is sans-serf or Gothic, sans means without, and the letters have no embellishment. This style of letter developed during the Gothic period and that is where it got its name. There is one other use of the name Roman pertaining to type that sometimes causes confusion. Slanted type is called italic, but straight type is sometime referred to as Roman. So when an editor notes, make Roman to a line of italic type, they are not saying to add serfs, they are referring to making the type straight by remove the italic.

The following examples show Roman and Gothic fonts. However, some decorative fonts are hard to classify as to serf or sans-serf and are simply referred to as Art or Display type.

Examples of serf or Roman Fonts

Garamond

Times Roman

Palatino

Examples of sans-serf of Gothic Fonts

Arial

Century Gothic

Tahoma

Examples of Display Fonts

Brush Script

Giddyup

MATISSE

French Script

A few of the fancy fonts are so difficult to read when they are set as all caps that must be avoided or used only as caps and lower case.

EXAMPLE OF ALL CAPITALS TYPE THAT IS DIFFICULT TO READ

Assembling letters of a font into words, it is called setting, thus typesetting is the process of formatting a manuscript for printing. When font letters come together, the kern is the space between the letters. Adjusting the space between letters becomes kerning. The power of typesetting software is so efficient that in most cases you will seldom have to worry about kerning.

This line of type is the same as above, 12 point Georgia but instead of automatic kerning, 3 point of kerning has been added between letters expands these lines.

This line of type is the same as the preceding, 12 point Georgia, but now condensed by minus 1 point kerning from normal.

When type was assembled the space between the lines of type were controlled by adding thin pieces of lead and the space between lines of type are known a leading. As you work with your cover type, adjusting leading is one of the controls you will most likely use.

This line of type is the same as above, 12 point Georgia on 14 point leading but this sample has been leaded out to 20 points.

This line of type is the same as above, 12 point Georgia but this sample has been leaded minus 2, at 10 points, something that was not possible with hot type.

There are rules about mixing fonts, weight and size, but if you will follow the simple concept of readability, I don't believe you have to worry about all these rules. I'm concluding this chapter by saying, play with various fonts, leading and kerning, practice and experiment.

A PASSION FOR TYPOGRAPHY

In the summer of 1974 I participated in a two week workshop on book design with Ansel Adams in Yosemite National Park. There were participants from around the world.

One evening a small groups of us were gathered at Ansel's residence to enjoy a glass of wine and chat. At some point, the conversation got on the topic of type design. Ansel pulled a type sampler from his bookcase and started pointing out some of his favorite typestyles. I watched as he ran his fingertips, over the lines of type as if caressing the letters.

Ansel was so particular about the type used in his books that after the photographs were printed by an offset lithographic process he developed, the type was added by letterpress in a separate pass through a letterpress printing press.

Chapter 3

PHOTOGRAPHS AND ILLUSTRATIONS

There is an old story about a man that took a violin to a pawnshop to sell, the pawnbroker said it was a cheap students violin and not worth much. Then an elderly man visiting the shop stepped up, took the violin, tuned it and began to play. Everyone stopped at the beautiful sound that came from the violin. "See," the man said, "it must be a Stradivarius and worth a fortune."

"No." The elderly man said. "It's an inexpensive student's violin just as the pawnbroker said. I'm the concertmaster at the symphony. In the hands of a master any instrument can perform well."

When applying this lesson to photography, the photographer makes the photograph. But like a professional violinist, the instrument plays an important role. That is why professional photographers spend thousands of dollars on their cameras. While a snapshot from a cell phone camera might look great on a computer screen, it doesn't mean it will translate well to a printed cover. The quality of the lens affects the clarity of the image. The resolution and dynamics of the image will reveal its quality when converted to print. If you intend to take your own photographs, you need more than beginner's knowledge of photography and at minimum a high-end consumer's camera.

If you do not take your own photographs, you still need to know what makes a good cover photo. Just as composer doesn't need to know how to play every instrument in the orchestra; they need to have a working knowledge of all of the instruments to use its voice effectively in their composition.

QUALITY

To begin with, to use a photograph for your cover it must be digitize. A photograph that is a transparency, slide or a print, will require scanning. Digital cameras create images ready to use in your design software. The camera must be 6 mega-pixels or greater. It should take the photographs in RAW, TIFF or high resolution JPAG at 300 DPI and at least 3000 x 2400 pixels. A few years ago, only professional cameras met these requirements. Today many of what are called consumer cameras meet and exceed this standards, and by the time this book is published, I am sure there will be even greater advancements.

The next essential your camera must have is a good quality lens. This is where some consumer camera falls short. Cameras with interchangeable lens like Nikon and Canon offer a full range of high quality lens, but there are new cameras with good quality lens, image stabilizers and sufficient speed to produce cover quality images. Research your needs and abilities, and then find the best camera for your budget if you plan to take your own photograph.

THE DYNAMICS OF A PHOTOGRAPH

We all know a photograph can convey a lot of information. So the first thing that must be considered is what the picture will say and how relevant it is to your story. Connect a key theme, location or character from your book to the cover photograph.

The next element you need to consider with a cover photograph is where you are going to place the title and author's name. The title should be prominent if not dominate the cover, not an afterthought stuck on the top or bottom of the photo. This means that the photograph must balance with the cover typography. Move the subject right or left and up or down to work with the title. When photographing a cover or directing a photo shoot, I usually make a thumbnail sketch of the cover and where I plan to place the type before I start.

When a cover photograph contains people, be very aware of where they are looking. If they look off the cover in any direction, it will lead the viewer's attention or eyes off the photograph. A slight look toward the title leads the eyes there and a slight look to the right leads the eye to the edge of the cover and into the text of the book. A subject looking directly into the camera is very engaging and if intended, sexy. Also, be aware of hands or fingers pointing off the page and in still-lives and landscape look out for lines that lead out of the photograph for the same reason. Finally, remember your color scheme before you shoot. Do you need costumes or prop of a specific color?

On romance covers, with two people in an embrace, have the subjects looking at each other. No matter how erotic the pose if one or both the subjects are looking anywhere but at each other, the message is less romantic. A couple entangled with one of the subjects looking into the lens is inviting the viewer to join the party. Subjects looking away from each other evoke danger, action, mystery, tension or discord.

A word about props, props are anything not human or background that interacts in some way with the subject or is the subject. Guns, knives and clubs are obvious in their meanings, but a camera, binoculars, maps, a bottle of pills or booze can tell stories too. Anything pertaining to or mentioned in the book are possible props for your cover photo. Whatever you use as a prop, make sure it is recognizable, not too small or confusing. You don't want the reader to ask, is it a bottle of medicine or poison? Make it clear.

One more thought on the use of props, are there obvious logos or product names visible? If so, do you have the right to use them on your cover? Get a written release before you use it on your cover. You might be told no, you can't use that product, but on the other hand, you might get some product placement money, that's better than a lawsuit after the fact.

Lastly, you will also need a written, signed model release for anyone and everyone that appears in the cover photography. If someone under eighteen years of age is in photograph, you need the release signed by the parents or guardians. Never use a model under eighteen in a sexually suggestive poses, you are asking for problems.

When using a photo service, review all your use rights and restrictions before you buy use of the photograph. That will include numbers of copies and in which countries the book can be distributed, as well as a verifiable model releases. If possible, buy a royalty free photograph. That means you buy the use of the photograph and not have to pay each time you use it. Photo banks are a great source for photos and art, but don't try to rip off their photo or take a photograph off the Internet or from another source without permission or buying the use rights. Get your usage right secured before you go past the thumbnail stage, availability of an image can change at any time.

Buying royalty free rights are not the same a public domain. Buying royalty free photographs means you have the right to use it without a per-use or impression fee, but you can't resale the photograph or art, the copyright still belong to someone else. Public domain means the art or photograph is no longer under copyright and you can use it without originators permission. Just because a photograph is in a magazine or on the Internet, does not mean it is in public domain. There are some gray areas with public domain photographs and art as to source. Newly reproduced collections of public domain art or photographs in a book or CD can be copyrighted as a collection, and if you take the image directly from that collection, you are violating the copyright. There are books and CD's of public domain art and photographs sold with the rights to use the art or photographs individually or as groups in your work, but you cannot sell the images for reuse. In these collections, usage is stated. If in doubt, ask.

CHOOSING PHOTOGRAPHS AND ART

Choosing photographs, illustrations and art is very subjective. My advice is to keep it clean and simple. Use the process of elimination, remove or eliminate anything that is not necessary. If you have multiple photographs or pieces of art to choose from, make mock-up covers. It is easy to do with Photoshop and print them with color inkjet print. I print my mock-ups full size on glossy photo paper. Then live with them a few days. Get opinions from others. Check how well they read from across the room. Take it to the bookstore and see how it looks. Ask the proprietor for their opinion, that's pre-publication marketing, who knows, you might book a signing.

Try variations and color combinations. Re-file each version you print with a version number and write it on the print. You will be amazed at how quickly you get confused as to which version is which. It is easy to make variations with

Photoshop, but if you don't save each variation as a separate file, it is equally easy to change the perfect cover and not remember how you got it.

Don't over complicate your cover. Keep it simple. Make it readable and you will create great covers.

MODEL RELEASE FORM

For valuable consideration, I, the undersigned, hereby irrevocable consent to and authorized the use and reproduction by

Photographer__________________________________
or anyone authorized by to you, of any and all photographs which you have this day taken of me for any purpose, without further compensation to me. All negatives, positives and digital images, together with the prints shall constitute your property, solely and completely.

Date______________________

Model Name____________________________________

Model Signature____________________________________

Address____

Parent of Guardian if under 18__________________________

Witnessed by_______________________________________

Chapter 4

COLOR

We humans have a large dynamic range of color vision. Through our evolution, we have developed color prejudice base on self-preservation. The study of color biases and their development are beyond the scope of this book. But, because of these there are some rules about color use that are better not broken unless you know what you are doing. I've mentioned some of these rules in the introduction and I will point out more as we continue.

WHAT IS COLOR?

Color is light vibrating at different frequencies. White light is the presents of all color, and black is the absences of all color. Though a cover may appear the same on a computer monitor and in the printed form, the physics of what you see is entirely different. The computer screen being generated light and the printed-paper being reflected light. It is mind boggling the amount of computer power needed to translate light images of the computer screen to print. So, if your printed cover doesn't appear exactly as your computer screen, understand that up until a few years ago the conversion was not even possible. Adobe Corporation and their Photoshop software played a major part in making this conversion possible for desktop publishing. Therefore, I heartily recommend using Photoshop or Photoshop LE as your minimum software for cover creation and Adobe's Acrobat for PDF file creation. A PDF file is the digital equivalent to camera-ready art. Photoshop and Photoshop LE, will allow you to output PDF files from the software.

So when you submit your cover and text as a PDF file, and receive your print proof, check the cover color carefully. The proof stage is where you need to make your final color correction. There will be some unavoidable color variation between your original and the print; it's the nature of printing. I use Photoshop CS3 on a computer with a color corrected monitor and find the proof print I make and the printed cover from my POD supplier are very accurate and there is little if any variation between orders.

PRIMARY COLOR

There are only three primary colors. On the computer screen, which remember, is light color, they are red, green and blue, RGB. In printed color, it is red, yellow and blue, reflected light. In our world, most perceived color is reflected, so from here on I will refer to reflected light only. Note that even though all perceived color is made of three colors, in printing a forth ink is used, black. Thus, full color printing is referred to, as four-color printing or process color printing.

SECONDARY COLORS

The three colors that are between the three primary colors are the secondary colors. Orange is half way between yellow and red. Green is between yellow and blue and violet is between blue and red.

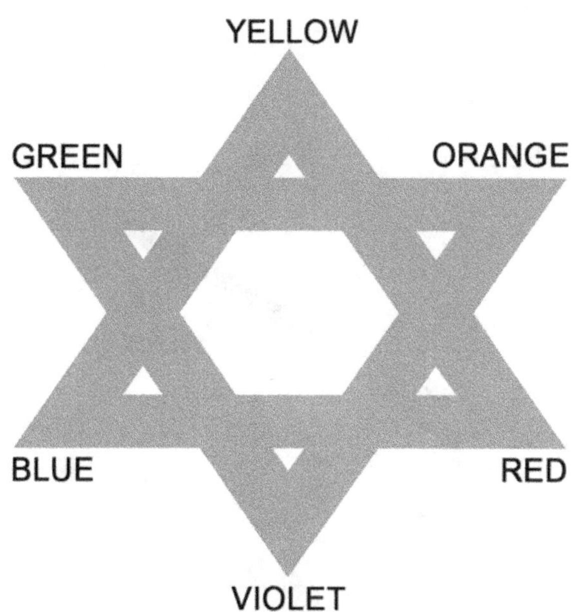

Illustration 1, The color wheel

THE COLOR WHEEL

A standard color wheel is created by using two equilateral triangles, inverting one and placing over the other, as shown. Starting at the top point of the first triangle and place the color yellow, then at the second point red and the third, blue and then on the second triangle, starting at the upper right point, place orange. That is the halfway point between yellow and red, and then on around violet is at the bottom point and green at the upper left point. There you have it a six-pointed color wheel.

If you then put a double-end pointer or arrow in the center of the wheel, the complimentary color is always directly across the wheel from where the pointer is pointing.

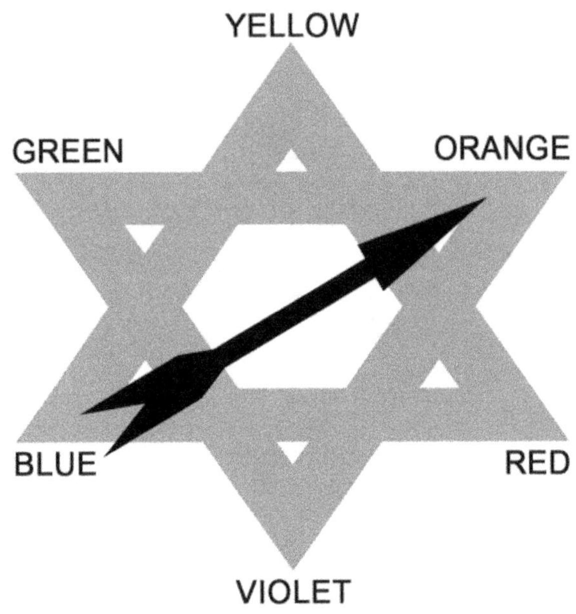

Illustration 2, Complimentary colors on the color wheel

COMPLIMENTARY COLOR

Complimentary do a number of things. First, as the name applies they complement each other. If equal amount of two complimentary colors are mix together they will make gray. Important for graphic, when complimentary colors are next to each other, they make the other appear brighter. When the complimentary colors are of equal saturation, intensity, they appear to vibrate. This is just the tip of the iceberg, but a good starting point as we start talking about color scheme.

A color scheme is a combination of colors that work well and look good together. Complimentary color schemes are very popular, red & green and orange & blue being the most popular. When red and green of Christmas are muted, reduced in saturation, think of adding white, they become the peach and teal popular in restaurant decor. Another interesting color scheme is called monochromatic, where all the color are very closely related to one color, using light, dark and saturation to create contrast. Split complementary colors are the hue on one side of complementary split to each side of the corresponding colors. An example is, when yellow is split to light tones of yellow/orange and sage green and are used to compliment violet.

Indiscriminately combining color can sometimes lead to color discord or clashes. Again, the use of the color wheel will help you out of such predicaments.

We have a built in feel for color, but the color wheel comes in handy when a color scheme isn't working or you want type that will pop. It also helps in choosing drop shadows and outlines for type.

COLOR AND EMOTIONS

This is where color theory becomes fun. Think of a color. I'll bet you can't think of a color without picturing an object. Let's say red, what do you see? Fire engine, fire, or a red balloon, and what emotions do you feel? Hot, danger, excitement and energy all come to mind and one image leads to another. There are the obvious connections to the color red, sex and food, and oh yes the stop sign. How then do we apply this to cover design? When you start marketing your book on the Internet you use a search engine and create a list of key words to use as search word. You want to tie the basic color of your cover to this emotional energy of your search words.

Even not-fiction works have an emotional thrust. Quickly write a list of at least twenty emotionally charged words that relate to your book. Is it sexy, hot, fast or cool, smooth, frightening or edgy? It might take some effort to get started, but soon you'll get in the swing of it, so don't stop at twenty, write your list until you're brain dead. Some of the last things that come to you may be the most emotionally charged. If you write with a partner, try doing the list first separately then read them to each other and see what new words the brainstorm session brings. For those that write alone, if you have someone who has read your manuscript, bring him or her into a brainstorm session.

Now that you have your list, condense it. Combine synonyms; look for the high-energy words. Reduce your list to four or five powerful or meaningful words. Think of the color each of these words evoke and write it down. You now have your color scheme.

Remember color is a powerful yet almost subliminal part of covers. Use it to your advantage. Some advocate going to the bookstore, looking at the area or shelf where your book will be displayed and doing something different. There is some merit to this approach, but being different just for the sake of standing out doesn't always work. A better design with a great composition, powerful graphics and emotionally charged colors will always standout more than the gimmicks, the odd size or inappropriate color.

Lastly, be aware of color trends. Stick to classic not the *In Colors* for this season. I would hope your book would be around for more than a season. Visit a used bookstore and look at the once trendy colors that now look old and tired. Classic color scheme and good design never go out of style.

Chapter 5

APPEAL

To sell a book, the cover must be appealing. A serviceable red cover with gold letters on a dictionary is appealing, red the color of sex and gold the color of wealth. Even if the subject of the book is less then appealing, it is the job of the books cover to be appealing.

When books were first bound together as pages as opposed to rolled up scrolls, covers were strictly utilitarian, to protect the precious hand written manuscript inside. As the wealthy and scholarly began to assemble collections of books on shelves, titles were scribe on the leather binding of the spine. Libraries became a sign of wealth and the book covers became decorated works of art encrusted with gold and jewels. However, with the invention of printing and increased numbers of books, book covers again became utilitarian. But with the development of dust jackets and paperback books, covers once again became works of art. And now those paperback books have evolved from a cheap book printed on inexpensive pulp paper to quality books, the cover are even more attractive.

Universally, several themes, colors and images are appealing to humans. Anything that related to our basic needs in a positive way is appealing. Food, well-being, comfort, wealth, health, happiness and without exception, sex, all stimulate the pleasure response. While culture will play a part on what and how we visualize pleasure, all humans seek it.

Of all the elements of a book cover, the title is obviously the easiest to generate a pleasure response. *The Joy of Cooking, Laughter the Way to Good Health, Think and Grow Rich* and the obvious, *The Joy of Sex,* are titles that immediately appeal to our pleasure response in any language, with a good translation. However, depicting these pleasures will vary greatly in different cultures. Food, a number one basic need for everyone, brings joy. A depiction of turkey dinner, for most Americans, is full of pleasure stimuli, but in countries that don't celebrate Thanksgiving or have and eat turkeys, the meaning is lost. So, knowledge of your market's customs, belief and culture is essential.

Some taboos when it comes to food are things like pork, forbidden in Israel, the Middle East and many Muslim nations. In some areas, even pigskin book covers are taboo, and India and Buddhist countries, are primarily vegetarian. You may not be designing your cover for foreign markets, but there are ethnic pockets in the U.S.A. that may have an effect on your sales. Identify your market, and then design with that market in mind. The real trick is to make your cover appeal to the widest market possible.

As I've stated before, sex sales. Beyond the need for food, water and shelter, nothing affects our daily lives more than the human sex drive. Without it, we would cease to exist as a species, but the human sex drive goes far beyond the need to procreate. The human sex drive can even override the need for food, water and shelter for extended periods. It can cloud judgment, cause others to break vows, commitments and laws, and even lead to death in extreme cases. The stories of the lovesick fool starving to death or meeting his demise at the hands of a jealous husband are common.

When I refer to sex in relation to cover design, I'm not necessarily referring to overt sexual content or images on a cover, but to covers that are sexually appealing beyond just color or title. A good example is the jacket and paperback cover by Michael J. Windsor for Dan Brown's, *The Da Vinci Code*. The deep warm red-brown background color with gold letters, are strong and masculine. The torn paper effect, a subdued subliminal phallic symbol, speaks of energy and urgency. The revealed mirror writing of Da Vinci says mystery, and the eyes of Mona Lisa exude sexuality, making the cover simple and sexually appealing.

The human form or as with *The Da Vince Code* cover, a small part, is always of sexual interest. The first thing humans do when they encounter another human is size them up sexually. We immediately determine sex, and then our primal instincts immediately establish, friend, foe or possible mate. This evaluation happens in a fraction of a second as part of our survival mechanism. Some would like us to believe this is more of a male thing. I believe it is an equally shared trait, but maybe a bit more pronounced or demonstrated in the male of the species because of men's assumed family protectorate role. I'm trying to be nice guys. However, the female is equally protective of her children, especially when a mate or protecting male is not present.

If it seems I am describing human nature as an animal instinct, I am, I want you to think of the sex action/reaction, as just that, primal, primitive and uncontrollable. All humans react to visual sexual stimuli. Most of the time, we don't even know we are doing it. Is it morally right to play on these instincts? As a designer, I don't believe we can avoid it. Just as we cannot avoid being judged by others as we walk down a street. Book covers are all judged using sexual criteria. If the cover is not sexually appealing, it is sexually unappealing; there isn't a middle ground.

Do I advocate using overt sexual content to entice sale? Certainly not, nor do I endorse subliminal trickery. Do I object to sexually provocative art and photographs used on covers? If the artwork or photograph is relevant to the book and market, I have no objection. I would rather the cover be a little offensive to someone than someone buy the book and later find the content offensive to him or her. I believe the cover artist and designer should accurately represent the content of the book using all the tools and their talents to sell the book and a sexually appealing cover is part of the job.

APPEAL IS SUBJECTIVE

Many images may be appealing to some and terrifying to other. My daughter is terrified of snakes even photographs and drawings. She would not pick up a book with a snake on the cover, much less buy it and bring it home. She will not tolerate an image of a snake on a book cover, even if it is face down on a table. The thought terrifies her. Another friend is so paranoid about snakes, she can't visit natural history museums because they might have a preserved snake or photograph on display. Certain images and symbols can be so universally threatening that entire countries reject them. Be cautious and test market your cover before publishing.

Chapter 6

BASICS OF BALANCES

Professional artists struggle with compositional balance in every artistic endeavor, but don't let that intimidate you. There are a few simple rules that will make your cover designs look professional. This chapter will focus on Type Balance.

TYPE BALANCE

When I started in the graphics business, Cold Type, the forerunner to Desk Top Publishing, was in it infancy. Fresh from Design School, I was hired to bring the new technology to a commercial print shop. I faced a group of old-time printers that only used Hot Type. Hot type, though beautiful when composed properly was limited. It was very difficult to do many of the things we take for granite today, such as slanted lines of type, vanishing points and curved type.

At present a graphic designer has so many variables available, it is mind boggling to say the least. With today's computers and software, the options are limitless, and that is where the problems lie. Just because you can do it, doesn't make it right, so I believe the old acronym KISS, Keep It Simple Stupid.

There was a time in the 1990's, when magazine and newspaper began to shift from linotype to computers and desktop publishing, that the layout and designs got so poor that many publications were unreadable. Slanted type, new typestyles, reverse leading and drop shadow were everywhere. The years of training that was once required to set type were replaced by anyone with basic computer skills. Finally, the realization that readability trumps creative freedom was embraced.

The examples I'm going to work with are in book format, often referred to in word processing as portrait, taller than wide, as opposed to album format, or landscape. While most books are in portrait format, the same principals apply to landscape.

Before desktop publishing, designers would consult type manuals of hundreds of typefaces and spec the type, to be set by a typesetter. These professionals would work with ridged mechanical parameters, especially before the advent of cold type and photolithography. Cold type allowed the designer to cut and paste lines of type that were impossible with hot type, opening new doors for graphic designers.

With current software and computers, we can select and change style at the click of a mouse. We can shrink and enlarge, angle, curve and distort type to our hearts content. Whether that's a good thing is sometime questionable. The computer is just a tool, not a judge of good or bad design.

So let's look at balance. There is nothing mysterious about the principle of type balance. Think of a seesaw, I hope the old playground standard isn't too obsolete that it no longer serves as an illustration. If you have equal weight on either side of the fulcrum, you have balance. As basic as these illustrations appear, they are the foundations of balanced composition that must be addressed in every cover design.

FORMAL BALANCE ON A SEESAW

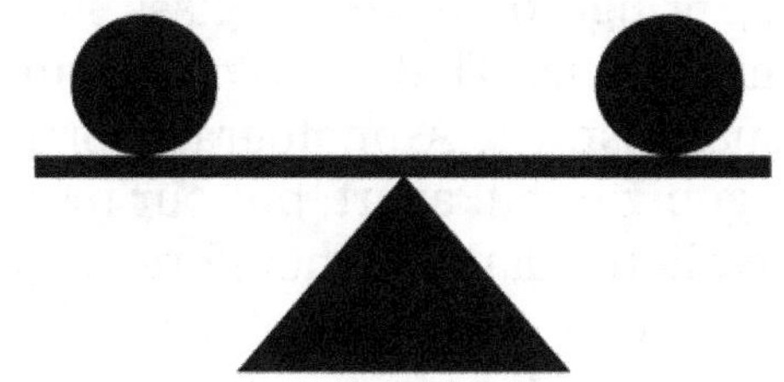

This is an example
of formal balance
as seen in simple
centered type

Illustration 3, Examples of formal balance

Though it looks simple and with today's computer typesetting, centering lines of type are as easy as highlighting and clicking center, but in the days of hot type, centering blocks of type took time and careful mathematical calculations.

Why balance? We human like balance. In fact, we demand balance. It probably stems from walking upright. We couldn't get out of our bed in the morning without balance. Balance is the thread that permeates everything we do. However, on paper, in photographs and in graphics we can create imbalance without much consequence. On the other hand, a house, bridge or drinking glass not balanced will have disastrous results. That survival instinct for balance affects our visual instinct. A photograph or piece of unbalanced art isn't going to fall apart, but our instinct says it will and we try to avoid the danger. Therefore, book covers, along with art or printed matter that is not balanced, makes us feel discomfort and we avoid them. For books, that may translate into lost sales.

Chapter 7

THE RULES OF COMPOSITION

In the last chapter, I discussed formal balance. The cover is balanced by placing the type and graphic on the centerline of the cover, the fulcrum with equal weight balanced on either side. So in the art and graphic jargon, we say the composition is *symmetrically balanced.* A cover, however simple, is a composition. It not only has balance, but movement. Movement on a formal covers takes place because of the typographic, we read left to right, top to bottom.

Formal composition is seen in architecture, in its formal building, temples and monument. They keep our interest because they are in a natural asymmetrical setting. Formal art and cover design, on the other hand soon become less interesting and somewhat tedious. The simple cover has been around for a long time, and is practical and functional, but not the most exciting. However, there are times when practical and functional is better than exciting and if that is your requirement; a simple formal cover is all you will need. However, to kick it up a notch, as the celebrity chef says, we need to add some spice. The spice being graphics, photographs, fancy typefaces, movement and color, but just as with a great stew, balance is the key non-ingredient, ingredient.

When we start moving an element off the centerline, our composition becomes unbalanced and something else has to be moved or added to restore the balance. This form of balance is *asymmetrical balance* as in the examples below.

INFORMAL BALANCE

So far, we have looked at horizontal balance, left and right on a fulcrum. In graphic composition, there is a form of vertical balance as well called proportional balance. Placing elements that are heavy high in a composition appear top heavy and ready to topple. Therefore, weight placed high in a composition need to balance with weight lower in the composition.

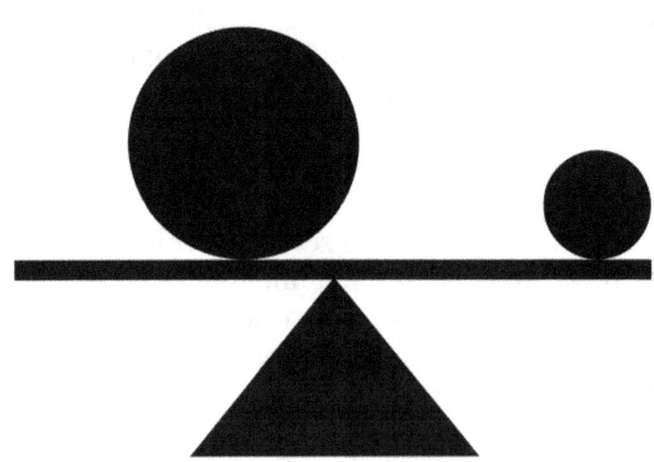

Illustration 4 Informal Balance on a fulcrum

Western artist from the time of Classical Greek have used a simple formula often referred to as the "Magic Thirds" or the "Rule of Thirds". Da Vince's Vitruius Man demonstrates these mathematical proportions found in the human form. For cover composition the easiest was to use this, is by visualizing a grid of nine equal sections. This theory proposes that placing elements of weight on or at the gridlines or at their intersections, will achieve balance and a pleasant composition.

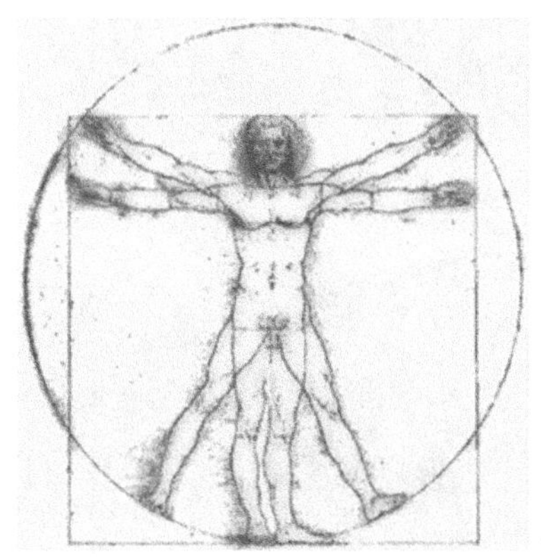

Illustration 6, Vitruius Man

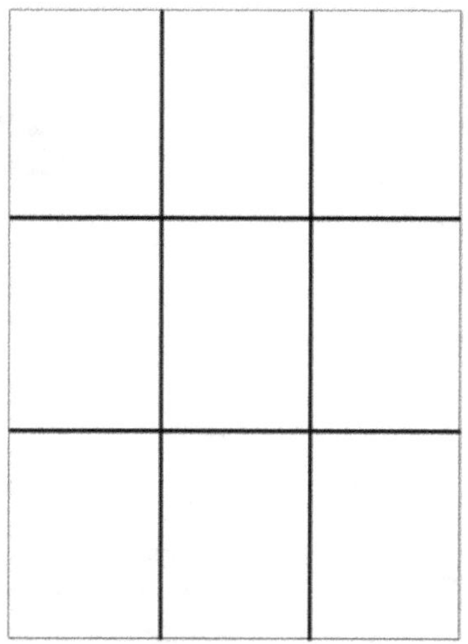

Illustration 7, Magic Thirds Grid

MOVEMENT

The final element of composition is movement. Our eye see with focus on only a small portion of whatever is before us, therefore our eye, focus points, is in constant motion over a composition. Look around you and see how small a portion of your vision really is in focus.

In the West, we read left to right, and just like we read, our eyes inter a composition in the upper left corner and scan down to the lower right corner. To keep a person engaged in the composition, you want to keep their eyes in the composition. This is achieved by leading the eye, once they reach the lower right corner, back up to the upper left where they entered the composition, thus scanning the composition repeatedly. In art and design, it's called, capturing the eye.

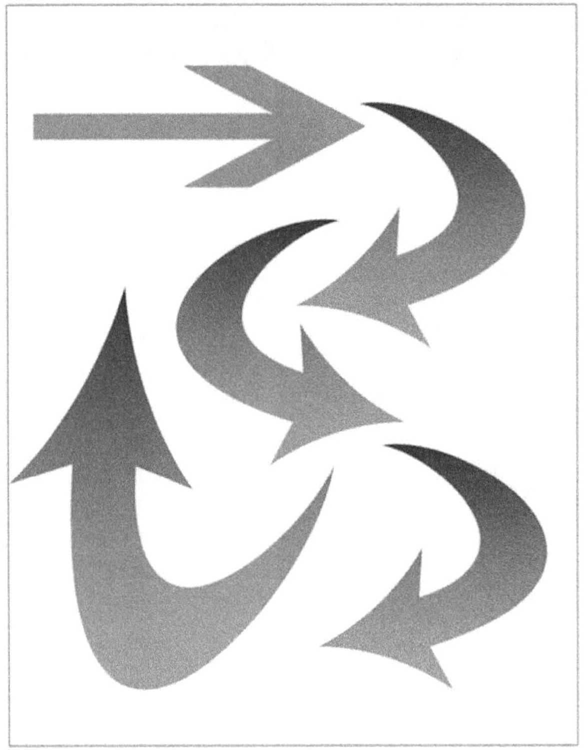

Illustration 7, Movement

I am concluding this chapter with an example of an informal balance design. Again, it is a simple cover with three blocks of type and a small graphic. The heavy title is high center with the graphics centered directly below. The authors name shifted to the left balances with lower block aligned to the right. Even though the block is lighter face and smaller type, being farther right and low, it balances the composition. I will show a redesign of this same copy in a later chapter.

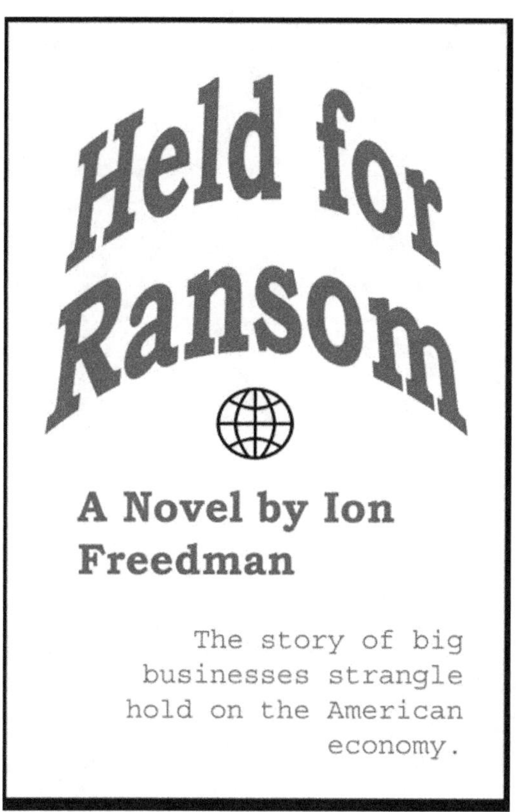

Illustration 5, Sample of Informal Balance on a cover

NOTE: *Compositional movement is flopped for audiences that primarily read right to left.*

Type, graphic elements, photographs and even the edge of the paper can lead the eye around and through the composition. The longer you can keep the viewer's eye, focus, attention, on your cover the greater the chance they will choose your book to read.

Chapter 8

BUILDING A FRONT COVER

Beginning in the late 1980's, I began using computers for my design work and soon the drawing board, X-Acto knife and pens disappeared. The only carryover that I still practice is creating thumbnail sketches, miniature drawing of my design idea with pencil or pen and paper. I use lined note pads and any writing tool handy. The crude sketches are approximately two by three inches in size, drawn fast and simple. It is my way of thinking on paper and I might make dozens of sketches with notes before I go to the computer and start composing. You don't have to use my method of thinking on paper, but you will need to develop your own mental shorthand to make notes of your preliminary design thoughts. In the following examples are my final three thumbnails that I will make into finished covers using Photoshop LE.

THUMBNAILS

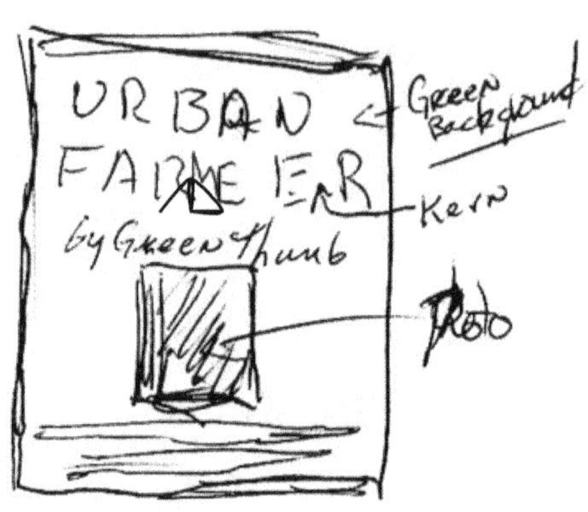

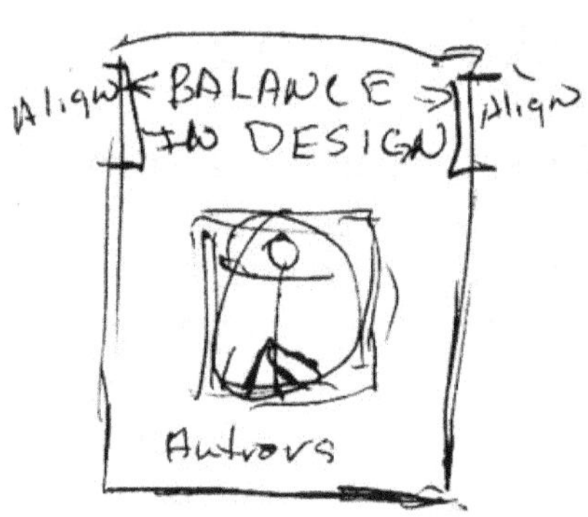

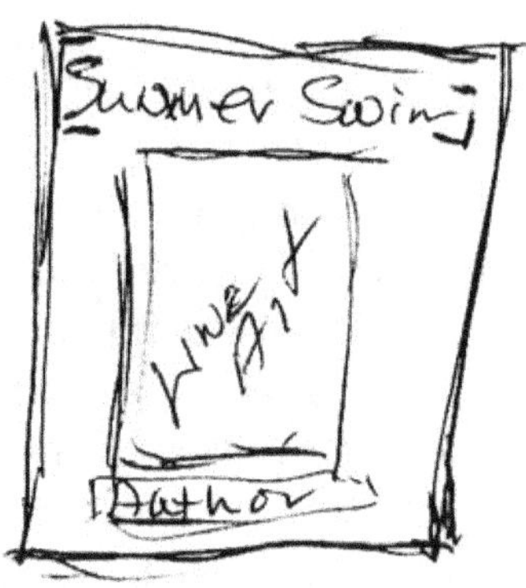

Illustration 9, Samples of thumbnails

DESIGNING A COVER

I will take you through my thought process of the three covers, explaining the design concepts. While they are basic formal designs, they are interesting and effective, giving you sound foundations to stimulate your own creative juices. Take what is on these pages and make it your own.

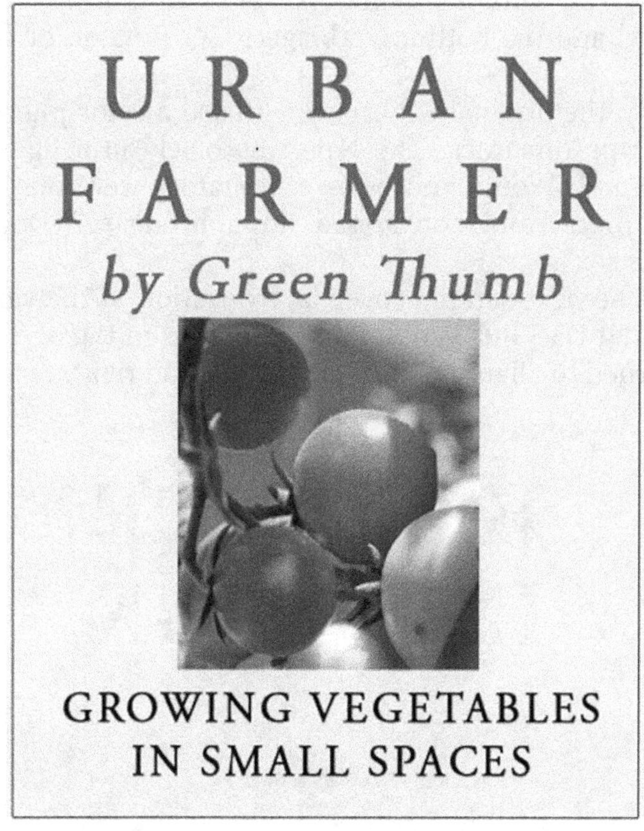

Illustration 10, Urban Farmer Cover

The first cover is a variation of a classic dust cover that dates back to the 1920's, Kahlil Gibran's *The Prophet*. You can look up the book on Amazon and see an example. It is simple, a title, authors name, an illustration and a block of verbiage at the bottom.

For my example, I created a gardening book, with title and author's name, photograph and verbiage. In my variation, I set all the type in Garamond. To make it more contemporary I set the title in all caps and put an extra space between each letter. You can achieve the same effect by expanding the kerning if your design software offers that feature. The author's name is set with normal spacing, italicized and the bottom verbiage is set Roman, or without italic.

In the original color cover, I used a color photograph of red ripe tomatoes. The type was black on a light green background. Would you believe, tomatoes were once called *Love Apples,* and considered an aphrodisiac? Does that count as sex appeal?

The next sample cover is a variation of the same design using Da Vinci's man and three lines of types. The title was kerned to align the lines of type left and right.

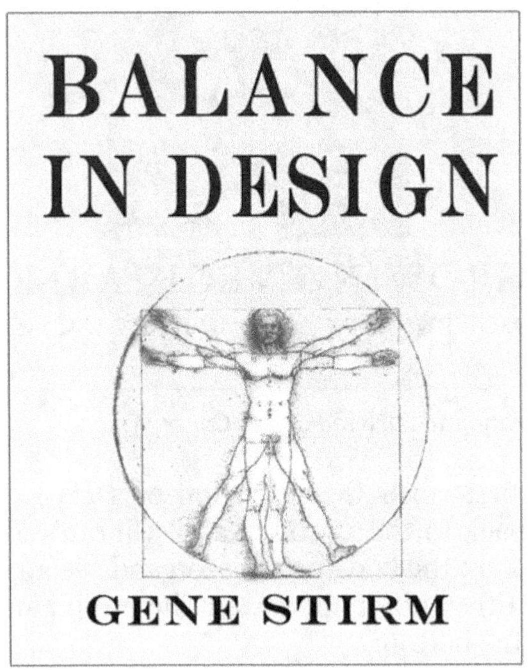

Illustration 11, Balance in Design Cover

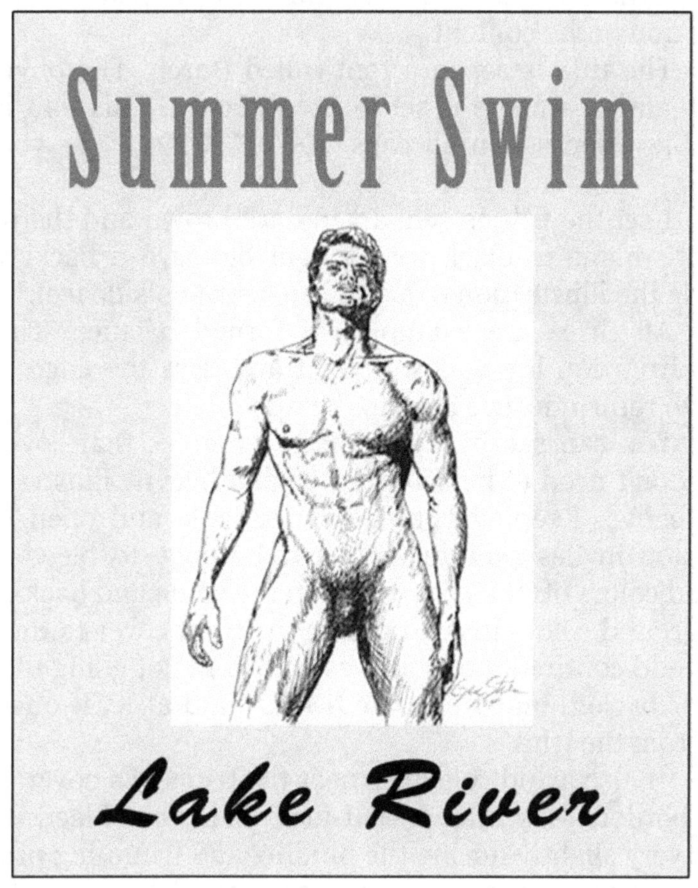

Illustration 12, Summer Swim Cover

Illustration 12, is for a summer romance novel. I chose a sexy, provocative line drawing that would be acceptable. Nudes in art, like Da Vince's nude male, Vitruius Man, and other drawings or paintings of nudes are often more acceptable then nude photographs. I wanted the cover to be simple, eye-catching and mysterious. The book could be a sexy romance, murder mystery, a gay theme story or a number of other possibilities. I designed this cover to force the reader to pick up the book and look at the back or inside to get an indication of the content.

The title is set in a font called Burch. The obviously phony author's name is set in Brush Script. This font is not readable when set in all caps. LAKE RIVER, as you can see.

I set the title in red, art in dark brown and the phony author's name in black with a light blue-green background outside the illustration to give a beach or poolside feel.

All three are examples of formal balance. The eye reads from top left to lower right and uses the edge of the book to return the eye back to the upper left.

You can see by these three examples that cover designs don't need to be complicated and heavily illustrated to be effective. Keeping your cover readable and open is the first step in designing a great cover. I like to bleed background colors off the trim and onto the spine and back cover. Background colors that flow from the front cover to the back cover add continuity to your design. If I'm not going to bleed a color background I end the background at least one-half-inch from the trim.

I also avoid rule lines near the trims of a cover, along with borders less than a half-inch wide that bleed. Cover trims very slightly during the binding and trimming process. The signatures, pages, of a perfect bound book are folded and gathered and then the folds at the spine are ground away and the cover is hot glued to the guts, holding the book together. The book is then three-knifed, trimmed three sides. All this is done in an automated machine. That is why even the best binderies will experience some variation, knowing this; you can avoid borders and lines that will emphasize these deviations. The thin outside borders on all the cover examples are to show the trims and do not print.

Chapter 9

THE COMPLEX COVER

Moving from the simple formal and informal cover designs, we begin to explore the more complex covers using informal balance. With it, balance and composition become trickier and require more attention. The next cover I will look at is for a hot and steamy Romance novel. From the brainstorming, the criteria for the cover are a strong masculine design using gothic type and a photograph of a sexy male figure. We don't have a photograph and the design budget does not include a photo shoot. A typical photo shoot would start at around $400 for the first four hours and go up. A model could add another $200 to $400 to the cost.

THE PHOTO BANK

A photo bank is a catalog of photographs produced by freelance photographers and easily accessed on the Internet. The category index can be very large, so it will take some navigation. You can do your own online search for photo banks of stock photos, or go to www.dreamstime.com, for a list of suppliers. I've used iStockphoto and have been very happy with their service and their prices are good.

Searching some of these sites before you have a need can be fun and interesting. It can even be a source of inspiration during brainstorming. Keep track of what interests you. I have found photographs that sparked ideas, but when I was ready to buy, I ended up spending a great deal of time trying to find the photograph a second time, I learned to make notes of the service's name, photographer and catalog number.

Once you find the ideal photograph for your cover, you will need to purchase the rights. Non-exclusive rights are less expensive and when you start cropping and adding type, you make it your own anyway. The chance of someone else choosing the same photograph for the identical purpose is slim, but if the idea of someone possibly using the same photograph on their cover troubles you, then spend the big bucks and hire a photographer and model or buy exclusive rights.

To buy photographs through most online photo banks, you have to set up an account first, and then buy credits. You have to use credits to purchase the use of the photograph. With the use price so low, I understand the need for a minimum purchase. At the time of this writing, the minimum number you can purchase is 12 credits, for $18.25. Remember to get a photograph as large as you will need for your cover. If your cover is 6 X 9, you need at least that size photograph and if you are going to crop the photograph, it will need to be larger. Buying a larger photograph and reducing it will not decrease the quality, but on the other hand, enlarging a photograph will. Also, you want an image that is at least 300 dpi. You have the option to buy the size and resolution needed at the time of purchase, the larger the photograph the more credits.

CG IMAGES

There is another way to obtain images of posed figure for a cover. There is software called Poser by Smith Micro. It produces computer-generated images of which you manipulate into infinite varieties of poses. I see some figures generated with this software used on published book covers and have even used some myself. Even though the manufacture advertises, no post work needed, I found myself spending hours in Photoshop manipulating the images before I got it to where I was satisfied. For my preference the figures are a little to perfect, so I had to rough them up a bit, add lens flair, and blur to blend with the background. If you are going to produce several covers, want total control of the art, have the computer skills and don't mind the extra effort, it's a good way to go.

YOU NEVER KNOW WHO IS GOING TO CATCH YOU

Several years ago, I designed a wine list cover for a large Las Vegas hotel and casino using one of my own photographs. The client asked to see a high quality proof of the photograph along with mockup. After sometime, the project was returned, rejected. Several months later, I was in Las Vegas and happen in that particular hotel. To my surprise, they had a new wine list using my photograph. When questioned, they insisted they bought the rights from a photo bank. I informed them that I had taken the photograph and owned all rights. They ended up paying me twice the originally price I asked for a one-time use for the photograph. Busted.

THE THUMBNAIL

With criteria in mind and the title, Sex Machine chosen and knowing I want to use a stock photo, I start a search for a possible image. I wanted to find one or more photos before I created thumbnails. When I find a possible picture to use, I copy the online image and save it. It will have watermarks, security marks or the word SAMPLE, in the image. My intent is simply to use the image for positioning, checking composition and pictorial evaluation. If the photograph works in a thumbnail, I purchase the image and go on to the finished art.

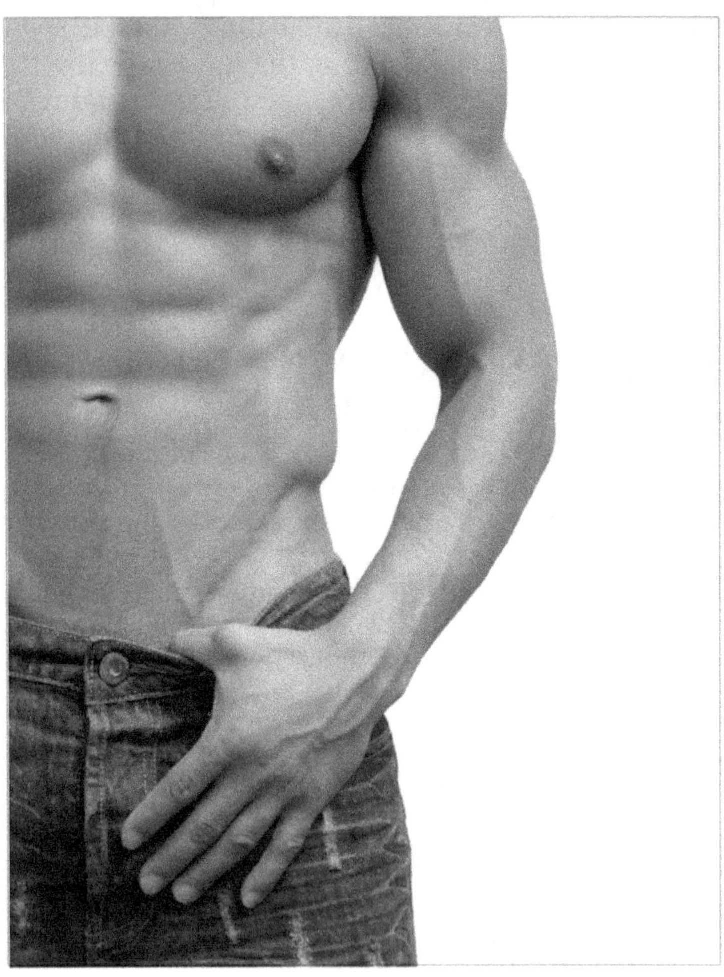

Illustration 13, Sample of iStock photograph

What I do when using photo images is make several small three-inch high prints on plain paper and sketch in the type for my thumbnails. When I am happy with my thumbnail, I buy my image and I work it up to full size. I develop my front cover first, in Photoshop. My personal preference is to make up several variation of my front cover and print them on glossy photo paper. I then show them to my wife and others for evaluation. I may hang them up in my office for several days. It's like finishing a manuscript; it's good to let it rest awhile before you start editing. This is also a good time to start gathering the information and elements for the spine and back cover, which I will discuss in detail in the second part of this book.

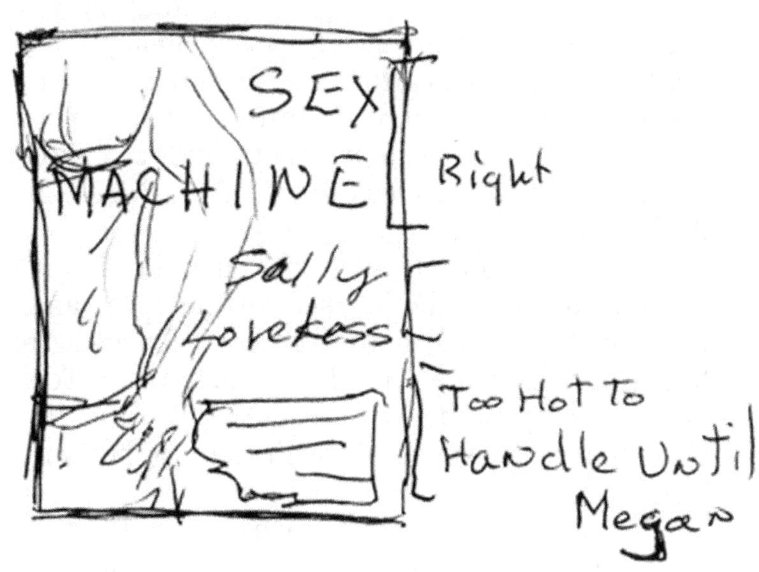

Illustration 14, Sample of Sex Machine Thumbnail

As I take my rough to finished cover, I know from the thumbnail that I need to mask out the background of the image to extend it to the right. If I was working with a plop-and-drop cover makeup program this would not be possible, again, Photoshop to the rescue. Honestly, I don't get a commission from Adobe. From my thumbnail, I was aware that the type that overlapped the image would be difficult to read and I had to manipulate it to make it stand out. I wanted the word SEX to pop, but the same size, style and color of the word MACHINE.

In Photoshop, I set the size of the cover with a quarter-inch bleed top and bottom and on the right side. The cover is a 6 X 9 finished trim book, so I set my size in Photoshop at 6.25 inch by 9.5. Remember to set your resolution at 300, and your color mode on, RGB Color. I find it best to use RGB color and let the printer convert the file as needed. This is a larger margin then required by some printers, but it's better to have extra bleed then not enough. I set up trim mark showing my quarter-inch bleed next. Photoshop LE 4, doesn't have a guideline feature, so you can use the grid future under view, you don't want your type cut off because it was too close to the bleed. Remember, there is no bleed on the left side.

Now, on a new layer, I placed and positioned my photograph, touching the left side of the cover and extending through the top and bottom bleeds. Since the photograph background is white, I used the Magic Wand Tool to knock-out the background and filled the background layer with fill color that now extends through the top, bottom and rights bleeds.

I next added the type, each block in its own layer to allow manipulation and fine-tuning of placement. The viewer's eye enters the design in the upper left at the models chest and is lead to the first word, SEX, of the title that was set as large as possible and fitted to the photograph. The rest of the title, the author's name and the verbiage, also balances with the photo and designed to lead the eye down the cover. Finally, at the word Megan, the eye lingers a moment before the subtle descending stroke of the letter g, turns the eye back to the models chest, and the entry point. This maintains the balance; leads eye through the composition and at the same time entices the reader to open the book.

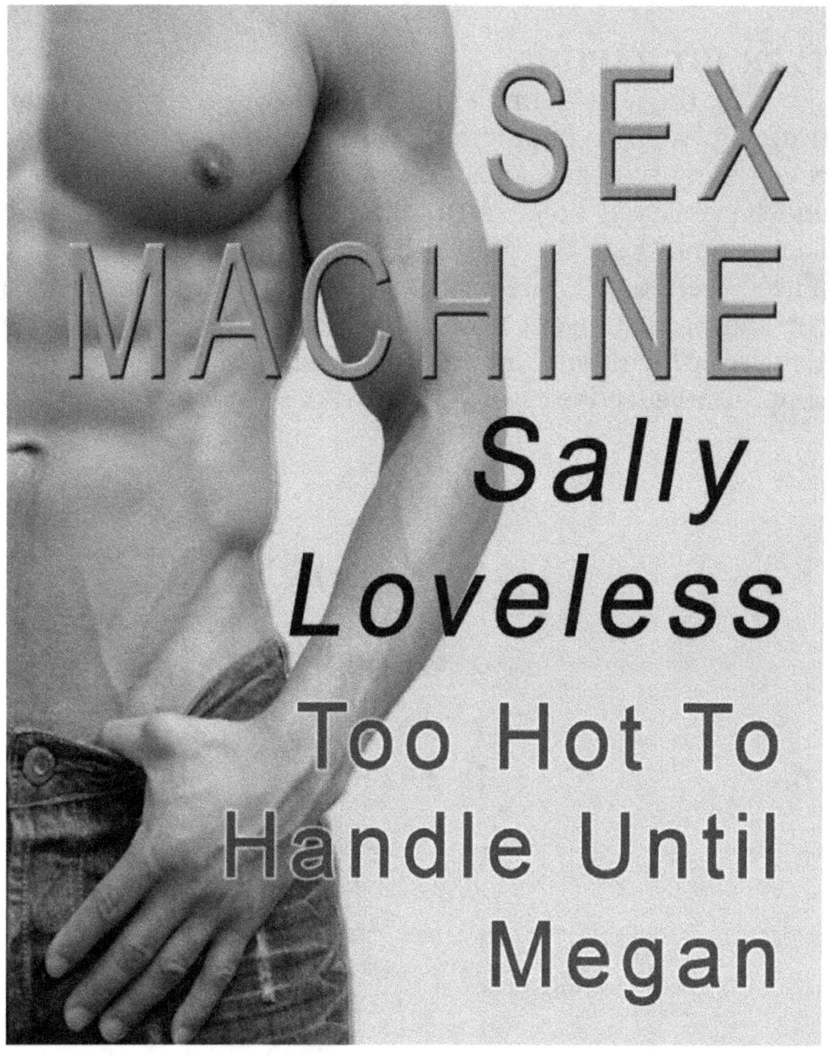

Illustration 15, Sex Machine Cover

When I am satisfied with a cover, I make a color proof print on my jet printer. I keep my master in Photoshop and then save a flatten Photoshop file, TIFF file and a high quality JPAG file as well as a lower quality JPAG file for the web.

TYPE AS GRAPHIC

In the next example, I used the cover copy from illustration 5. With no photographs or illustrations I redesign the cover using type and a cookie cutter shape from Photoshop and an enlarged dollar sign, skewed filling a money green background. I set the title with random fonts and sizes and placed them on a white shape, skewed to make it look like a cut-and-paste ransom note. The rest of the copy I set in Courier, which looks like a typewriter face. This makes a simple and effective cover.

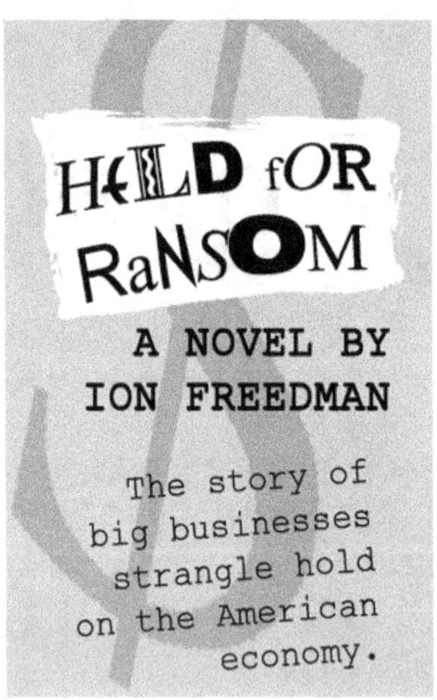

Illustration 16, Held for Ransom Cover, second version

PART TWO

Chapter 10

THE BACK COVER

MARKETING

To this point, we have focused on the front cover of a book as a hook, something to entice a reader to look closer, which, in the bookstore setting means to pick up the book and read the back cover. If your book is a hardcover, it means reading the back of the dust jacket. This is where the marketing truly begins.

I know selling and marketing isn't every author's favorite pastime, in fact, most authors hate it. However, in today's market, even successful authors with their books published by big publishing houses with a large marketing department must get out and sell their books. For the independent self-published author it is imperative. The self-published author must have a marketing plan, website and take time away from writing to market their books. Just posting your book on Amazon isn't going to sell it.

I have stated before, the book cover is a critical part of your marketing. The cover doesn't need to be designed until well into the writing process, but should not be put off until the last minute. You should have a completed representation of your front cover at least three months in advance of publication for use in prerelease marketing such as posters, website postings, advertising, bookmarks and so forth. Then make final tweaks before the book goes to print.

A full marketing plan is beyond the scope of this book, but all the elements developed for the back cover should be an intricate part of your marketing plan and strategy. Resign yourself to the fact you will have to market and sell your book and yourself. Plan to spend at least one full day a week marketing in the form of book signings, book festivals and personal appearances, even if it means walking around a farmers market and passing out bookmarkers. Then add at least an hour a day for correspondence, networking and planning. This amount of time cannot be past off to an assistant or spouses and must be incorporated into your writing schedule.

MY AVERAGE DAY

My day starts between four and five A.M., I have a three-cat alarm clock. After herding cats, each want in or out of a different door, I settle in with my morning coffee and read at least two hour. I read fiction, non-fiction or research, whatever is near. Writers must be readers. After breakfast, I head to my office. Jazzy, a Siamese cat, usually beat me to my chair. She thinks she is my secretary and I wouldn't dare tell her otherwise. I spend the next hour or so reading and answering mail and e-mail. I'm not a great blogger or into social networking, but in the writing/publishing business you have to stay connected, and since we now live in the country, I don't have many face-to-face contacts so I do use Web to stay connected. After a morning coffee break with my wife and a discussion of the day's agenda, I either return to my office or go to my studio.

I do the heavy computer work like book formatting, cover designing, illustrating, graphic and developing marketing pieces in my office. I have a laser printer for hardcopies of my manuscripts. I proof and edit better from hardcopies. I also have a large format inkjet printer for color proofs and marketing pieces. My office also contains my files, copier and reference library.

The studio is a detached 8 X 12 room, heavily insolated, nearly sound proof and separated from the main house. There is no phone. The window looks over our small town and the Southern Sierras beyond. This is where I write. Nestled in a comfortable chair I use a laptop to write and I am only disturbed if it is truly necessary. I strive for a solid four hours a day of writing, four days a week. Research is on top of that, and general business duties take up another day. As a writer, I work, 60 plus hours a week. I put in a couple of hours of yard and house chores weekly and I usually cook the evening meals. My wife has her own alteration business and helps with marketing and copyediting. In the evenings, we take walks or participate in water aerobics. I put in a six-day work week, if not at home, in the field. I love camping in our 13 foot Scamp, fiberglass travel trailer and with my laptop in hand, I spend the days relaxing and writing. Usually one day of the weekend is spent marketing at book festivals, farmer markets, book signings or whatever may come along. My life and work has always been in the creative arts, it is my joy and pleasure. I don't have a problem being motivated, if anything, I don't have enough time.

GATHER YOUR THOUGHTS

When I get a story idea, I try to get notes on paper as soon as possible, even if it means getting up in the middle of the night and writing down the idea. I don't know how many great story lines have passed through my head and gotten lost because I didn't make notes. When I start to revisit the story idea and feel there is a possibility for a book, I start a binder, I buy one-inch binders in quantity at Costco. I have a bookshelf for book idea binders. As soon as I start developing the book, I keep research notes, outlines, character notes, plot points, photographs of location, characters and the like in the binder. I prefer binders because I can start with a one-inch binder and move the contents to a larger binder as they fill. When I start writing drafts, I keep a hardcopy of the draft in another binder and move the project to a works in progress shelf. I keep hardcopies of two or three drafts. Even though I persistently back-up my files, I have had power outages and hard drive crashes and because I had hardcopies, I could reconstruct my work.

At about the second draft stage, I get serious about titles, covers concepts and marketing. All this information goes into another binder. I work on more than one project at a time and when I get to a sticking point in one, I don't just stare at the screen until something happens. I go back to my idea shelf and revisit the binders of ideas. I have on occasion incorporated older ideas into a current book.

Another way I use my binder system is as a filing system. I keep notepads strapped to the arms of my reading chair with elastic bands so I can make notes. My reading chair is also where I watch TV and there are often programs that I make notes about. Once or twice a week my notes make it to my office, I reread them and if they are coherent, date them and file them to appropriate binders. I also keep to-do lists on the arm of my chair, the butt of a lot of family jokes.

When the time comes for me to begin designing my final cover and start planning the marketing, I have binders full of things to start with. I even keep files of covers I like as idea starters, a habit left over from my advertising agency days. At the agency, we had files we called morgues, full of photos, printed advertisement, trade magazines, logos and even old presentations that didn't sell. In the morgues is where most the productive brainstorming took place.

This is how I work and I in no way want to imply you have to follow my procedure, however, you must develop an effecting way of working and filing ideas. You are a writer, which is your job, even if at the present time you write part-time. And especially if it's presently part-time, you must have good, well-organized work habits. At the end of the writing process, I keep a marketing binder and recycle the extra binders for the next book.

I have had people come to me and ask for advice on a book they are writing. When I ask to see what they have so far, the first problem I observe is that they are not organized. They have at best a folder full of notes, randomly tossed together like a salad. Their efforts consist of a day or two of feverish work every now and then and by the time they figure out where they left off the last time they worked on the project and what they need to do next, they have lost their edge, close-up the folder and wait for the spirit to move them again, someday.

I have worked on book projects over long periods, years actually, being able to spend one or two days a month writing. However, with a good outline and organized comprehensive notes, I can quickly refresh my thoughts and make productive use of my time. The old saying goes; talent is ten percent inspiration and ninety percent perspiration. To quote Steven Sondheim "A vision is just a vision if it's only in your head?"

Chapter 11

ELEMENTS OF THE BACK COVER

Just as there are elements for a front cover, so too are there elements for a back cover. The elements of the back cover can include a short description of the book, a bio of the author and possibly a photograph, along with readers' comments, awards, websites and other pertinent marketing material. Not all of these elements need to be on your cover, but as marketing tools, you will see how effective they can be.

BOOK DESCRIPTION

The description of your book is very important. Start with a one-sentence description; this is going to take some thought. Then write a description of approximately a page, an eight-and-half by eleven-inch page double-spaced. Now between the one-liner and the page description is the description that will appear on the back of your book. If you are happy with the one line description, wonderful, use it. Don't write a book to describe your book. In Hollywood, movies are sold by their one-sentence description.

This is a good project to work on while you're book is at the editor. If you are going to self-edit, it's a good idea to set your manuscript aside for a couple of weeks and work on your cover elements. Self-editors should give themselves time between the finishing of the manuscript and beginning the final editing process. Editing is different from the writing process and most writers should have an editor. Remember too that editing and proof-reading are not the same either, you need both. There should be at least three proof readings. Proof your manuscript before formatting, proof the galleys, the formatted copy as hardcopy, and proof the assembled proof-book, and always double check your proof corrections.

As you write your description, be aware of key words. There are keywords like adventure, romantic, thriller, sexy, mystery and suspenseful. Weave them into your description and use them as part your keyword search list. Try to incorporate your genre in your description. Also, suggest age or maturity and hint if there is profanity or sexual content. Remember the romance novel is the largest selling genre and most are hot, sexy, and often laced with graphic sex. If your book is a romance novel, you probably don't need to specify or hint at content unless you write romance for a young audience or Christian romance and there is no graphic sex or profanity, then note it on the cover.

Today, most novels have a sprinkling of profanity. In contemporary literature, moderately sexually graphic scenes as the story calls for it are also expected. A hint of this in you marketing with words like crusty, sexy, romantic, raw and sometimes violent will warn readers in case this in not their preference in books. However, if your book deals heavily in sex and violence, a statement stating so should be on the cover. The same holds true for works about the paranormal and alternate points-of-view of religious, sexual or political views. Don't be deceptive about the content of your book. If you are pushing a particular belief or life style, say so on the cover, you will never get true converts through deception. Include words like paranormal, mysterious, otherworldly, extrasensory, telepathic, intuitive and psychic on the cover or words like Christian, liberal or conservative views.

AUTHOR'S BIOGRAPHY

You are a writer, and yet your own biography is the hardest thing your will have to write. Start by getting it all down, from birth to now. This does not need to be a book, but don't limit yourself at this point. Fill in every important detail, including dates, locations, education, professional credits and full name of important or famous people you've worked with or know.

My work as artist and actor has put me in contact with many famous people, but early in my career a friend, Sandra Carson, asked me to autograph a tablecloth that she then embroidered over the signature and used it for special dinners like Thanksgiving. I recognized almost every name, John Wayne, Dennis Morgan, Lee Marvin. John Raitt, and dozens of other famous actors. Sandra was actor/comedian Jack Carson's wife. She informed me that only people she knew signed her tablecloth. She emphasized the word knew, distinguishing between an acquaintance and someone she knew. An acquaintance was someone she had met, someone she knew was someone she had spent time with and actually got to know. I now understand what she meant; you can meet many people in a lifetime, but get to know only a few.

MANY BIOGRAPHIES, MANY LIFETIMES

Once you have your master biography, keep it in a file. You will return to this master biography from time to time to make updates. This biography is not the one you print and send out, it's the one you edit to your needs. When I say edit it to the needs, I don't mean falsifying it. You may require a short, tightly edited biography for a book signing or a press release and a longer more detailed one to accompany a review copy of your book. If you have a diverse background, you may want to highlight only the parts of your credentials that pertain to the subject of your book. My biography that accompanies my works of fiction doesn't necessarily cover my years of work in printing and graphic unless the book has something to do with the trade. Similarly, the fact that I am an ordained minister and Shaman, has little relevancy to this book. Keep your published biography as brief as possible, relevant and interesting.

As you write your biography, you will want to write it in both a first-person and a third person perspective. Most people like to read a short biography in a third person format. It eliminates the line after line of I, I, I. When I am interviewed for the press or a magazine, I give the interviewer a copy of my complete biography, so they have my basic information. This is also the version of your biography that you would give an agent or publicist, who will in turn, edit and rewrite it before sending it out. Keep a copy file of every version of your biography. Make notes of to whom you sent it, so that when you do updates you can sent them a revised version. A writer's biography is like an actor's headshot. It must be short, sweet, to the point, professional and carried with you at all times just like a business card.

COMMENT AND QUOTE

Another element that is nice to have on your back cover are comments and quotes about your book. This is achieved by sending a manuscript to a carefully selected group of friends and colleagues. Tell them it is a preview copy of your new book and that you would appreciate comments about the book. Give them a deadline on when you need their input. Ask them to make their comments in writing and give you written permission to use their comments for marketing. Don't promise that you will use their comments; the use is up to you. However, whether you use their comments or not, give them a signed published copy of your book as a thank you after publication

BAR CODES

The last element that must appear on your book is your ISBN bar code. ISBN's are numbers issued from Bowker. If your book is going to sell through any retail market, it must have an ISBN and bar code. Some POD such as CreateSpace will provide you with an ISBN. This may be fine if you plan to publish one title. One of the main drawbacks is, the printer owns the ISBN. Don't confuse the copyright with the ISBN. If the printer owns the ISBN and you change printers you simply have to get a new ISBN, and your book becomes a second or revised addition. A POD or printer may call themselves a publisher, but as a self-publisher, you are the publisher.

As a self-published author, I recommend you buy your own ISBN. A single ISBN from Bowker can cost more than $350, however a block of ten ISBN's cost about the same so you only pay $35 each. You can save the numbers and use them as needed for other edition and titles. They don't expire. This will require that you set up your own publishing company. Don't let this frighten you; it's simple and relatively inexpensive if you in live in the U.S.A.. If you live outside the U.S.A., you will need to look into that country's laws. In the U.S.A., you will need to make a fictitious name filing in the county in which you live. If you live in a city, you also need a home-based business license. All of this will probably cost around $300 if you do it yourself. You don't need to incorporate; you can simply file as a sole proprietor. My wife and I are the sole proprietors of Way West Productions. Most distributors will require a Federal tax ID number and states will require a Seller Permits if you sell at book festivals and on-line. You will need a Seller Permit anytime you sell directly to consumers in states that charge sales tax.

I will defer any further discussion to the many books on the subject on the business aspect of self-publishing.

Most large book printers will create your bar code when you supply your ISBN. If you own an ISBN, I recommend you let the POD or printer create the bar code; it will save you from problems. The bar code is not the ISBN, the ISBN its part of the bar code, there is other information in it, and I don't read bar codes well. If your printer cannot generate your bar code here are some sources; Bowker provide ISBN and bar codes, www.bowker.com; Bar Code Graphic provide bar codes only, www.barcode-us.com.

Now with your front cover designed, executed and in a TIFF or JPAG file format, all the elements of the back cover ready and a thumbnail of your entire front and back cover in hand, let's assemble the camera-ready art. Oh, did I say thumbnail? Yes, you should make a thumbnail before you start the actual cover assembly or mechanical.

BACKUP SO YOU DON'T HAVE TO BACK UP

In my opinion, you can never make too many backup files of your cover or manuscript. I use flash drives and backup several times a week. On the first of the month, I make CD backups of everything I worked on during the month. I seldom loose data, but have had disc drives fail or have accidentally deleted files. I also make a hardcopy printout of my work.

Chapter 12

DESIGNING THE BACK COVER

I believe that you should have all the elements of your back cover written, your photographs ready and any other information that will appear on the cover in hand before you begin designing. With these elements in hand, you may have to start severely editing. Don't be disappointed if you have to eliminate some of the elements, you will use them later when you are marketing your book.

The only difference between creating a dust jacket for a hardback book and a soft cover for a paperback is the dust jacket offers additional space for bios and other elements on the flaps. I am going to proceed designing a paperback book cover. If you are working on a dust jacket, simply remember to use your flaps.

Earlier in this book, I talked about looking at front book covers, and that you should collect copies of the book covers that are striking to you or covers that you like. The same is true with back covers, but I recommend you keep them separate. Don't let a front cover you like dictate how to layout your back cover.

As a writer, you probably have an extensive home library of your own. If not, a simple way of collecting back covers is go to your local library and look at books. Pull a half-dozen that you like and make photocopies. They don't have to be in color. If there are certain interesting color combinations you like, make a notation on the copy, otherwise you will work with your color scheme from your front cover. You can repeat this process until your quarters run out or the librarian chases you out of the library for making a mess.

Back cover designs run from simple, minimal designs to overcrowded and confusing. You may want to separate back cover photocopies you've made into stacks of, I really like, it's okay and what was I thinking. Don't throw the cover's you don't like a way. You need to keep examples of what you don't like as well as what you like.

Now, with the stack of, I really like this cover, try to determine what makes that design likable. For some the simple minimal cover appeals to them. Others may find they like or require more information on their back cover. Spend some time with this exercise it will reward you greatly.

No, we are not going to copy somebody else's back cover, but we don't have to start from scratch on the project either. Choosing a sample that you like, see if the elements you need on your cover will fit. If they don't fit, can you make them fit? Or what if you have to cut a particular element because of space, how will it affect the entire design? Now, take a sheet of paper, draw your back cover to the dimensions of your book, and block in the elements.

You will use this layout sheet as a mechanical design to compose your back cover in a word processing or design program. Once you have your layout, you will quickly see which elements need editing, usually shortening to make it fit, and what elements might need more embellishment. For most of us, elimination will be in order.

Learn how to create your own Dazzling Book Covers with this Comprehensive Guide by Veteran Cover Designer, Gene Stirm.

With the growth of Print On Demand Companies and Mega Online Bookstores, Self-Publishing is a viable option for a great number of today's writers.

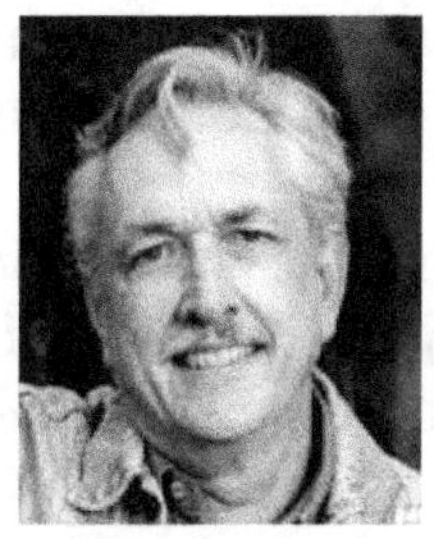

California artist, graphic designer and writer, Gene Stirm, lives in Tehachapi, California. After finishing art school in 1971, he began a career as a graphic designer. In 1973 he was hired as Art Director for Josten's America Yearbook Co. He later started his own printing and design company in Orange County California, with clients including The Fairmont Co. & The Plaza Hotel, NY, NY. Gene conducted workshops and teaches art, graphic, marketing, photograph and Photoshop. He is a student of Native American art and culture, Shamanism and the author of the novel, *Mystical Path to Mystique*.

Every book deserves a great cover. It is the number-one marketing tool for the Self-Publisher.

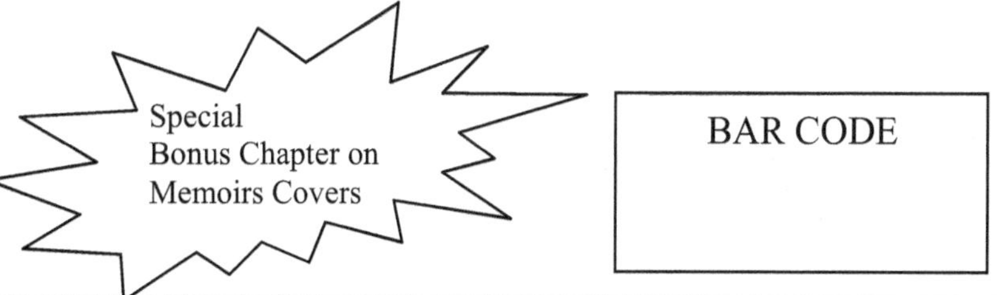

Illustration 17, back cover layout using a word processor

You can experiment with type sizes. I tried to make the most important elements of the back cover readable without my glasses. Depending on what you want to emphasize, you can make some of the back cover blocks of copy as small as nine-point type. If you are using a photograph of yourself or a graphic, keep them small. The large full back cover photograph of the author is somewhat out-of-date at this time. Remember to tie the back cover type styles to your spine, front cover and interior of your book.

Using my type layout sheet, I rearranged my copy and placed a shape to emphasize the blurb about memoirs, which I made fit in the final art. I moved blocks of copy around until I got it to read the way I wanted. Then when I was ready to make up my final cover, all my back cover copy was in one place. I did not include testimonials or reader comment. I may on a revised version. Compare illustration 17, with the actual back cover of this book to see the evolution of the design.

Remember the back cover of your book is where you say the things you cannot on the front cover. This is your marketing tool. This may be the only time you can speak directly to a perspective buyer. It is very valuable space so don't waste it. But at the same time don’t overdo it either. Give your back cover some air by not making it solid type. Use blocks, different color type and simple graphic to break up the page.

Chapter 13

BUILDING THE FULL COVER

In this Chapter, I will take you through the steps of assembling an entire book cover. I will use as an example the book you are reading. Not many years ago, the graphic artist would makeup art boards of the cover to send to the printer, these boards were called mechanicals or camera-ready art. A few printers today may still require art boards in the form of mechanicals. However, all major book printer and POD printers use computer generated art and PDF files for cover submission. Therefore, I will focus only on preparing your cover for digital submission.

I will cover in detail the selection of your printer in Chapter 15. I use the term printer to refer to the entity that will actually produce your finished book. Remember, as a self-publisher, you are the publisher.

Many book printer and POD suppliers such as CreateSpace, have cover creation software available. However, for this book I am using Photoshop LE to assemble and product the final art as a PDF file for submission.

THE COVER TEMPLATE

To this point, I discussed all the elements of a cover design individually. These elements will work for both book covers and dust jackets with at most minor modification. Now with your cover design decisions made, and having a thumbnail sketch, your back cover copy placed and proofed in your word processor mockup and all art, photographs and ISBN in hand we, are ready to put it together. But, before you can, you will need a template.

A template is a mechanical layout of your cover. It is your blue print or foundation of your book cover. It shows the margins and bleeds, the placement of the ISBN and the exact dimensions of the spine. Do not try to estimate these figures yourself. I have been making up templates for book covers for forty years and would not presume to know the requirements of a print shop without knowing the equipment to be used and having a sample dummy book of the exact paper to be used made up first.

You cannot make-up a cover template without knowing the total number of pages of your book and the trim size. You cannot know this until your book, called body or guts, is formatted. Books are printed in signatures, the flat sheets of paper before it is folded. The absolute minimum number of pages in a signature is four and can go up to 32 or 64 or more pages, depending on the size of the printing press. The multiples are always in units of four and usually run between 16 and 32 pages determined by a trim size. You should know the number of pages in the signature your printer uses. If your book is 181 pages and the printer only prints on 16 page signatures, the printer will add blank pages to the back of your book, in this case 11 blank pages, to make a total of192 pages, 12 signatures of 16 pages. If you know there will be blank pages as you format your book, you can use these pages for marketing or other information. You will have to pay for these pages; you might as well use them.

CreateSpace printed this book. It is an industry standard 6 X 9, perfect bound paperback book. If you plan to sell your book though, Amazon, bookstores and distributors, use Industry Standards sizes. Industry Standards must also have a minimum of 48 pages.

STANDARD TRIM SIZES
5 x 8 inches
5.06 x 7.81 inches
5.25 x 8 inches
5.5 x 8.5 inches
6 x 9 inches
6.14 x 9.61 inches
6.69 x 9.61 inches
7 x 11 inches
7.44 x 9.69 inches
7.5 x 9.25 inches
8 x 10 inches

CreateSpace uses 24 page signatures. Do not argue, CreateSpace equipment is set up for a 24 page signature; it would not be practical for them to offer any other configuration. The total number of pages for this book is 120; including title page, dedication, content index and other back pages. By going to CreateSpace's, Creating Your Cover File, and submitting my trim size and total number pages I was able to download a custom cover template in a Photoshop file with instruction.

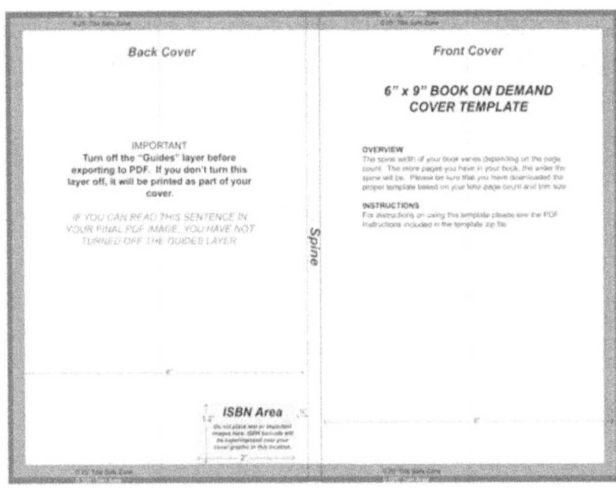

Illustration 18, Sample template

Your printer should provide you with a digital template or exact measurements for your cover. In CreateSpace's template, the spine, margins and ISBN area are clearly marked. You simply assemble your cover in layers on top of the template, turning the template layer on and off as needed. Remember to turnoff the template layer completely before you make your PDF file to submit the cover for printing.

If your printer only supplies you measurements, be very exacting as you make up your template, possibly have them check your rule-up before you assemble your cover.

BUILDING THE COVER

For the cover art of this book, I wanted to show some of the example covers used in the book along with some of my own favorite covers. I wanted to assemble a collage of covers, sometimes called a scatter page. I knew the art would be busy and possibly fight or distract from the title. My plan was to create the art first, but with a clear idea of type placement.

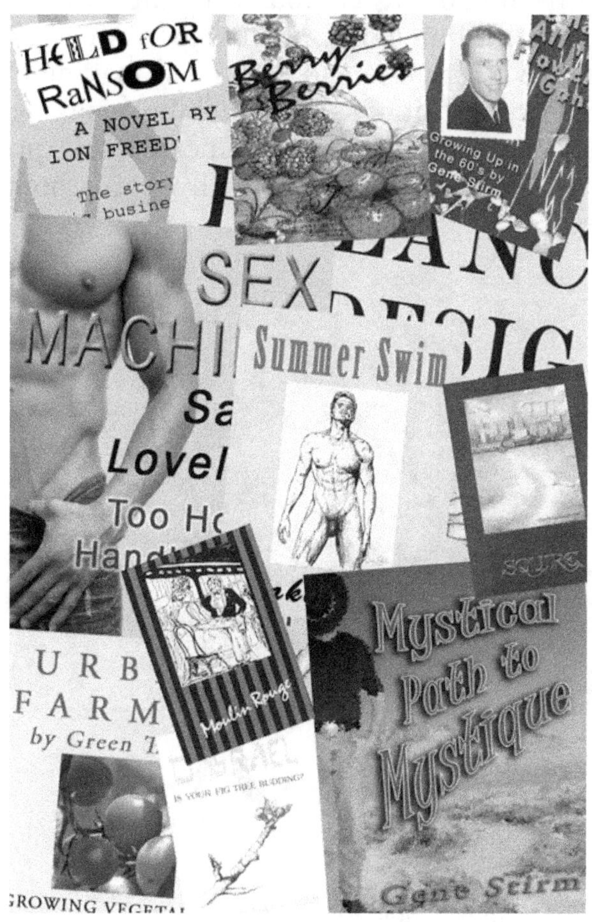

Illustration 19, Cover Art

I started by bringing all my chosen covers in to Photoshop and then sized and rotated each cover into place, balancing color and weight into a pleasing composition. Once I had the collections of covers placed the way I wanted,

I flatten the layers to a single element. I next placed my title, subtitle and name, each in new layers. I tweaked the color and sizes of the type and added shadows. Using Photoshop filters; I softened the focus and lighten the art. When I got it to where I liked in on my computer monitor, I printed a high quality inkjet print on glossy photo paper. After studying the proof, I made a copy file and continued making changes to enhance the composition and readability, making separate file copies after each change. I repeated this process ten times over two days; coming up with what I thought was a final cover.

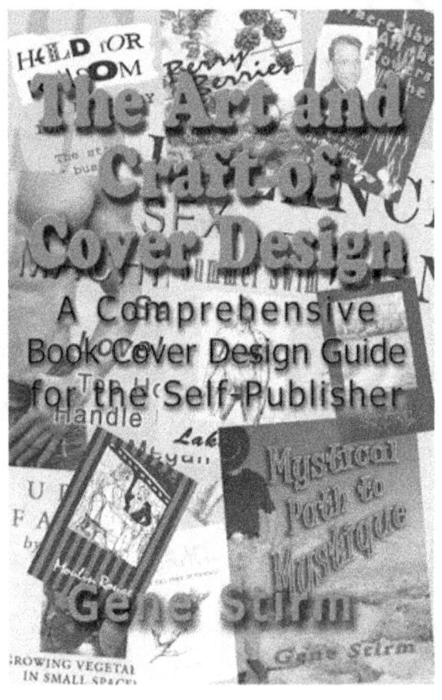

Illustration 20, first cover of book

I let the cover design set for a few days as I prepared the back cover. After looking at the cover for some time, I was unhappy with the readability of the subtitle. Trying some more enhancements of the type, I finally placed a block of transparent white behind the type, a technique called ghosting the photograph. To define the ghosted area better, I put a one-point rule line around the block. At last I had the front cover I wanted. I then make a flatten copy of the art and placed it on my template.

THE SPINE

The spine of a book is the space between the front and back cover where the book is held together. Saddle-stitched books do not have spines, but sometime have a small line of type run vertically near the fold on the back cover. The spine on a comb bound book can be printed, but it is expensive and rarely done. Printing on a spiral bound book spine in not possible. That leaves perfect bound and case bound or hardbound books. Book spines in the U.S. and Canada always read from top to bottom when the book is vertical and bottom to top in the U. K. The spines on some books are wide enough that the publisher or author's name can be run horizontality. The title should be the same or similar type as the front cover title. The spine does not need the subtitle, but should have at least the author's last name. The color of the spine ought to harmonize with the front and back covers and be readable from a few feet away. Don't set the spine copy so large that it looks crowded. A publisher's bug or logo can also be placed on the spine.

On perfect bound books, the spine can shift slightly during binding. CreateSpace recommends avoiding hard vertical separation between cover panels and spine. I try to use a color for the spine that blends with the front cover and wraps around to the back cover, softening the edges of the spine.

THE BACK COVER

I used a peach color background for the spine and back cover. Using Copy and Paste, I drop my word processor copy on my template, each block on a separate layer. I used red and black of the cover type for the spine and part of the back cover as well. CreateSpace made up my bar code from my ISBN. I left the space blank exactly as indicated on the template supplied. Do as instructed and don't put anything in this space, not even a background color. I supplied my own ISBN in the proper dialog box on the setup page and CreateSpace made up the bar code and placed it on the final cover. Being this is nonfiction book, I printed a classification line in ten-point type in the upper left corner of the back cover, Reference/Publishing/Cover Design.

THE FINAL STEP

Once I had my finished cover, I make three file copies, a Photoshop working file, a Photoshop flatten file and a PDF "Portable Document Format", file. The PDF file will be the file uploaded to the printer. I keep a working file in case I need to go back and change or update something on my cover later. It is difficult if not impossible to change a flatten file, but you need to flatten the file before you make your PDF file. Check with your printer for any additional specification and how they want the file named.

I have a large format printer that allows me to print the full size final cover. If you have a smaller printer, you can title and print your cover or print it in sections. Trim and proof you printed copy, really proof it, I see author's names miss-spelled on covers and not even the writer, who looked at it a dozen times caught the mistake until the job was printed. Proof, Proof, Proof.

When your cover is ready to submit to CreateSpace, fill in all the necessary information and upload your cover. If there are no major errors in the file and your ISBN is valid, you will be notified that your cover is accepted. This does not guarantee that there isn't a possible problem with bleeds or that something hasn't changed or been omitted in the file conversion or unloading process. You will have to buy a proof copy of your complete book and proof it before you push the publish button. Proof everything, from cover to cover again. Take your time and do a thorough job, you can't blame mistakes on the printer of publisher.

WRITERS AND BUSINESS

The most successful writer, artist, musicians and actors I have had the honor to meet and know, have all been very successful and savvy businesspeople. They are the CEO's of a company where their talent is their product. They may have agents, managers, personal assistances and publicist working for them, but they are in charge of their own careers.

As a writer, you need to be a businessperson, keeping an office with complete record and financial accounting. You have to know where your manuscripts are, what proposals are out or pending, and if copyrights are claimed.

You need to maintain a reference library, filing system and archive. You have to know your market, trends and your readers. And you must constantly hone your craft.

The fat patrons, that fed, shelter and took care of artist, have passed. Likewise, the days of writer's stumbling around the world in a half drunken stupor supported by their publisher, spitting out an occasional novel are gone. Today, successful writers are lean, mean writing machines.

Chapter 14

MEMOIRS

As the baby boomers begin to reach retirement age, the popularity of writing and publishing ones memoirs or autobiography is growing. And with the development of POD printing, the ability to self-publish small quantities of quality, inexpensive books is now within the reach of everyone. I'm not going to reflect on the reasons why someone might want to write and publish their memoirs. That is beyond the scope of this work. This chapter will focus on cover ideas specifically targeted to the memoirs and autobiographies. Of course, everything in this book pertains to designing a memoirs cover. Whether you are planning to produce a few dozen books to give to family and friends or dreaming of national distribution, good design is essential. Memoirs as compared to a autobiography usually focus on a smaller portion of the person's life and therefore using a photographs of the author or of the period make excellent starting points for a cover design.

I have to make a comment about self-publishing memoirs for a family member. I consented to edit a memoir written by an uncle. I usually shun such a project, but I had some time and I thought it would give me a chance to learn more of the family history. I edited the first couple of chapters trying to make it both coherent and interesting. It was not well written to say it nicely. I sent off a copy of my edited chapters and soon got them back. All the changes and deletions I had made were written back in the manuscript. There was a note criticizing my editing and displeasure with the changes and corrections I had made. It was obvious that my uncle didn't want editing, but an endorsement of a very poorly written manuscript. I packaged up the manuscript and returned it. I later found out that I was the fifth or sixth person to try and fix his manuscript.

Before you begin writing your memoirs, determine your audience, if it is for friends and family have fun and write, as you will. But if you intend a larger audience, have it edited by a professional. When you are close to your work or story, you don't see your mistakes and pitfalls. Be thick-skinned, willing to listen and except editorial criticism, it's of the work not you. Writing is a skill and a craft that takes years to hone. Change what is necessary to make the manuscript sellable. Remember too, that professional editing will not guarantee sales. Not every life story will be a best seller.

DEVELOPING A MEMOIRS COVER

Everything discussed to this point pertains to memoir covers. There is no special form or template for memoir covers. The only difference between a memoir cover and any other cover is whether you plan to sell it to the public. If you plan to sell your memoirs, you will need an ISBN for your book and a bar code on the back cover. If the book will not be sold, then ISBN and bar code can be skipped, however most POD services will require one.

In my example cover for memoirs, I am introducing a technique called a collage cover. I based the design on a memoir of a boy becoming a man is the sixties. I'm including a photograph of the author and memorabilia from the period including a yearbook. I used a flatbed scanner to create the artwork, scanning objects that were relatively flat.

You could use part of a poster, a theater or concert ticket, war metals, anti-war flyers or slogans, maybe part of a burnt draft card or a tie-died tee shirt. Make sure that you don't use copyrighted or registered objects without permission and if you use a photograph of someone other than the author and they are still living, get a signed model release.

This is a fun project. Assemble your objects. More than you will use. Give yourself some time to play with this. If you don't have a scanner, maybe a friend of family member has one you can use. Remember scanners require software and you will need to further manipulate the image and add type in Photoshop or other software. If you are using a graphic designer for your cover, this is a great project to work on together.

You will be working upside-down from behind and your image will be in reverse. You won't know exactly what you have until you make a preview scan. Once you have something you like, scan and save with the scanner set to 300 dpi or higher. Then do some more rearranging and make more scans. Make a print and visualize or draw where the type will go and see how well the composition is balanced.

DEFINITION OF A BASKET CASE

One day back at my drawing board, my sales manager call and asked me to meet him in the conference room. "I think you've got a basket case." He chuckled into to the phone. When I got to the room he had two large suitcases full of photographs and hand written pages open on the table. "The author wants you to make it into a book, cost is no object."

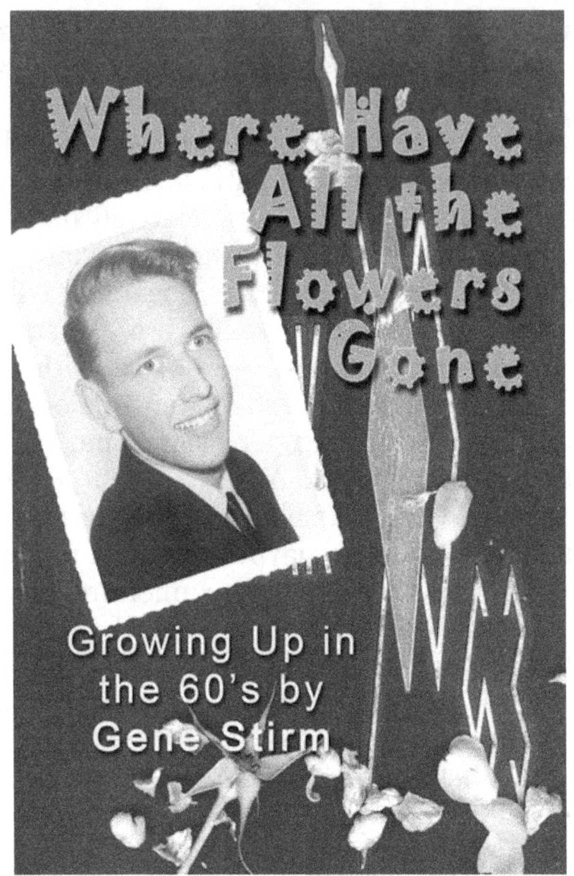

Illustration 21, Collage Cover

Before flatbed scanners were available, we made up a collage and photographed them with a large format camera. You can still do this with a good quality digital camera on a tripod. For some people it is easier to work face-up then upside-down on a scanner. The camera approach also works well with a larger object. It's hard to put the back of a car or a brick wall in a scanner. I have actually used this technique on a beach, with shells, starfish, driftwood and the title written in the wet sand.

Chapter 15

CHOOSING A PRINTER

I have worked with self-publisher for more than forty years. Some writer/publishers fit the classic mold of the Vanity Press variety. But I have met and worked with hundreds of self-publishers that made a very good living doing so. I'm not going into the reason why someone chooses to self-publish as compared to publishing through a royalty publisher. Many a self-published authors, after experiencing some success with the self-publishing efforts landed a lucrative publishing contract for their book. There are also royalty published authors that at the end of their contract have decided to self-publish.

CAUTION

There are a huge number of Vanity Publishers, also called Subsidiary Publishers, which will take your money and provide you at best a mediocre product and can end up owing your copyright and all your publishing rights. The self-publishing waters are full of sharks. Beware and do your homework before you sign any agreements and putting down any money. Read Patricia Fry's book, *The Right Way to Write, Publish and Sell Your Book,* and see the resource section of this book for more information.

THE DIFFERENCE BETWEEN COMMERCIAL PRINTERS AND SUBSIDIARY PUBLISHERS

The Vanity Publisher usually runs an advertisement saying they are looking for writers and guaranteeing your book be published—for a price, usually a very big price. They offer to do all editing and design work, for a price, and then print your book, usually a minimum of a thousand copies. Do you know how many boxes a thousand books fill? They may offer sales opportunities through their web-based outlets, for a slight additional fee. And if you don't want your garage full of books, they will offer a fulfillment service, again for a fee and warehousing fees, marketing fees, advertising fees and on and on, until you're drained dry. Oh, by the way, the copyright and ISBN they obtained for you, is in their name.

The latest twist on the Vanity Press game is Fee-Based Print on Demand. The only advantage to Fee-Based POD is you don't have a thousand books to store. Your contract however may still require you to buy a certain number books and if you want to get out of the contract your will have to pay them, or lose your home, some may take the dog and kids too. Stay away from all Vanity Publishers and Fee-Based POD.

A commercial printer, on the other hand will offer you a value service at a legitimate price. A commercial printer can run from the small corner copy store to huge commercial printers. Somewhere in there is the right printer for you. Today we have a number of POD printers where you can setup your book from an a la carte menu with truly minimum cost, the setup cost will depend on your knowledge and the work you are willing to do. There is no such thing as a free lunch.

If you are not computer literate or have little word processing and photo imaging software knowledge, expect to pay for these services to get your book formatted, cover designed and the project ready for the printer. Some larger commercial printers have in-house graphic design and typesetting services.

WHAT CAN YOU EXPECT TO PAY

The prices quoted here are ranges based on the current market. At present graphic design and printing prices are holding steady. Don't be afraid to ask for quotes. Shop around and expect to see samples of previous work they have printed. If you are on a budget, you may want to contact local colleges and design schools for someone that is just getting started in the business. They may not be timely and you will have to stay on top of the project, but you might end up with a real winner, or you might get what you pay for.

First, your manuscript must be in digital format. That means typed in a standard, professional word processing file. If it is not, you or someone will have to key or scan it into a digital format, this may cost up to $10. a page. Legitimate printer will not accept a handwritten manuscript unless it's possibly by Da Vinci, Leonardo that is. If your manuscript is hand written, there is no way to estimate the cost of having it typed.

EDITING

With a completed manuscript in digital form, typed in 12 point Times Roman or Courier, double-spaced at 25 lines per page, expect to pay for basic copyediting $150. to $400 for the first 10,000 word and $.015 to $.04 per word beyond the 10,000. That is for grammar, spelling, punctuation and consistency. For line editing, add another $400. to $600. and up.

Another possibility is ask a friend or make an offer to pay a schoolteacher with an English major to proof your work. A good editor must know common, usage and style. For fiction, it's best to hire an experienced line editor.

DESIGN

For a generic interior of a book, formatted with a standard template expect to pay between $375. and $500. For the placement of photograph and graphics, you could add $10. to $25. each. Make sure your manuscript is edited and well proofed before formatting. Changes after layout can be very expensive.

A generic cover, again from a template will run $350. to $500. and a custom cover design would start at around $1000. and special illustration could add another $1500. In the 1970's when I was working at Josten's Publishing, my design service were billed to the client at $50. an hour and when I had my own company some of my covers ran over $30,000. for a single design.

PRINTING

Once you have your cover and interior designed and ready for the printer, it is best to have two or three commercial printers bid on the job. If your book is a small, saddle stitch book, most commercial printers can handle the job, but for perfect bound and hardback books, you will want a printer that specializes in book printing. You will need detailed specs as to trim size, number of pages, paper and binding before you can get a price. Bleeds and crossovers, line, charts or photograph that run through the gutter from one page to the facing page add to the price as does color ink or photography. Printers will usually price the jobs at two or three quantities; say 1000, 2000 and 5000 books. The higher the quantity the lower the unit cost.

Paperback covers for perfect bound books should be UV coated and included in the estimate. Paperback books may also have foil stamping, embossing or die cuts.

The case bound book cover is usually simply cover cloth with foil stamping on the front cover and spine with the dust jacket having the graphic, copy and color. However, there is no limit to how fancy a hardcover can be, including embossing and printing, on silk or other fabrics and of course leather. It may include a slipcover as well.

PRINT ON DEMAND

Print On Demand, POD is a relatively new technology, though we talked about it in the 1970's. It can be laser jet, ink jet or digital print using ink and digital plates on anything from a desktop printer to a full size four-color printing press. It allows the computer driven printer, once the book is up loaded, to print and assemble a book with cover in any quantity from one book to as many books as needed. It eliminates producing and storing books before needed. A POD book can be ordered, produced and ready for delivered in 24-hours. The unit cost is higher than traditional printing, but for the small publisher selling 500 books or less of a single title a year, it is revolutionary. There are limitations at this time as to bleeds, crossover and physical requirements that POD cannot provide.

There are a number of high quality POD companies, Lightning Source Inc. and CreateSpace being two of the largest. Amazon owns CreateSpace. To work with commercial printers and POD companies you will need to setup your own publishing house as discussed earlier. I have used and am very pleased with CreateSpace. CreateSpace can supply your ISBN, which is fine if you plan on publishing only one book, but remember they will own the ISBN. You own the copyright and may cancel your relationship at any time with no further obligation.

Other advantages to POD are lower startup costs, easy corrections and revisions and you don't have large quantities of your books to store. The trade-off is a higher unit cost, but if your book sales take off, as the publisher you can switch to a commercial printer for larger quantity to reduce unit cost. And lastly, a royalty publisher may pick up your book, and since you own all rights, you are free to do so, even if the POD owns your ISBN. You will need a new ISBN anyway for the second edition, and third or fourth. Keep believing.

Whichever way you wish to print your book, check the quality of the work and ask for references. Do your homework. Learn the business. You wouldn't open a restaurant or repair shop without knowing the business, even if you were a great cook or could fix anything. A business is not a hobby. Learn the self-publishing business before you invest. Be a professional and make all of us self-published writers proud.

SOME DAYS

Throughout this book I've give you an ambitious model for a writer/self-publisher's life. There are times however, when the tide of daily life, family demands and need for creative expression turns into a title wave that comes crashing down on you.

When the computer crashes, the cat knocks over a cup of coffee on your desk, the toilet plugs up and is flooding the hardwood floor and you have been up since three A.M. trying to meet a deadline, you wonder what the—is going on. You stare out at the world completely overwhelmed. It happens to all of us.

That's when you take some, **Creative Lag Time**, that's what we called it, and run away for a day or two, maybe a week and renew that inner you. Refresh your creative spirit. You will soon be back at the keyboard, typing away and loving every minute of it. Writers write.

Chapter 16

CONCLUSION

With the rise of print on demand technology and online book sales, self-publishing has become a viable option for many writers. Even if you are not self-publish, I believe a writer should be proactive in every aspect of the publishing of their book, not just the marketing. Therefore, the writer must have at least a passing knowledge of every facet of the publishing business. As a self-published writer, you are a businessperson.

You don't have to be a mechanic to own a car, but some basic knowledge will keep you from being ripped off. A few years ago, I took my car to a dealer for an oil change and I was told I needed new brakes. My car had less than 30,000 miles on it and showed no outward signs of brake problems. The dealer then brought out a formidable looking document releasing them from liability, as they declared my vehicle unsafe to drive off the lot. I think they call that intimidation. I said no, stuck to my guns and left the dealership. With the knowledge I had, I was certain there was nothing wrong with the brakes. To make sure, I took my car to a brake and tire shop that I had dealt with in the past and trusted. My brakes were fine and I drove another 60,000 miles before I needed new brakes.

DEALING WITH SMALL PUBLISHERS

The likelihood of a new or unknown author landing a publishing contract with a large publishing house is slim. Most likely, a small publisher, if not self-published, will publish your book. A small publisher could be a sole person in a tiny office with no staff, and less than a half-dozen published titles. It does not mean that the publisher cannot do a good job for you, but you, as an author, must be aware of these issues. Ask questions.

- Has the publisher published other books in your genre?
- Who will edit your manuscript and how extensive will the edit be?
- Who will design your cover and book?
- Will you own the copyright?
- Will you keep or relinquish other right?

These issues can make or break a publishing deal. You must also consider advances, unlikely with a small publisher and new author. Your contract must clearly define royalties, distribution and marketing. An agent or attorney should review the contract. Also, check the solvency of the publishing company and talk to other authors represented by the publishing house. If the publisher is hesitant in giving you information in any of these areas, run, do not walk to the nearest exit. A royalty publisher will not ask you to pay any of the cost of publishing, except for possibly unnecessary changes you make after formatting, or if you make unreasonable demands. There is no negotiation after you sign the dotted line.

A royalty publisher, will do the design, format, print, distribute and to some level market your book. They may require you to do a certain amount of marketing, book signing, public appearances and interviews at your expense. They may suggest you hire a publicist also at your expense, but beyond that, they pick up the tab.

WHO WILL EDIT YOUR MANUSCRIPT

I discussed earlier, that in the publishing business, there are line editors and copy editors, you need both. The line editor will edit your manuscript line by line, checking clarity, readability, continuity, voice, and grammar, and making suggestions on content and so forth. They are the ones with the red pen that will slice and dice your manuscript. They may cut scenes and characters and rearrange timelines. You must be strong, though you may hate what they do to your precious baby; they are really your best friend. You can disagree with their edits, but look at their edits and suggestion closely and try it their way. If it isn't what you are trying to say, or not your style, then chance it back, maybe it needs to be somewhere in the middle. With some publisher, once you sign your publishing agreement, you no longer have much a voice in the editing process.

If your manuscript isn't full of red marks when it comes back from your editor, you either are a damn good writer or have a lazy editor. I would suspect the latter. I believe a new writer should have their manuscript edited at their own expense before submitting their manuscript to a publisher. You will never learn so much about the craft of writing until you have your work edited by a competent editor.

WHO WILL DESIGN YOUR BOOK AND COVER

If you are not going to design your own book, remember not every book designer is a cover designer or vice versa. A secretary with a word processor and Photoshop is not a book or cover designer. Small and even medium-sized publishers do not have designers on staff. Designers, like editors, are often independent contractors hired as needed. Be diligent through the design process. Be proactive, asked to meet with the designer then present your ideas clearly with examples of art or photographs. Nothing aggravates a designer more than someone saying, I don't like that, without comprehensive reasons why and positive input. This holds true whether you are working as a self-publisher or through a royalty-publishing house.

FEE BASED PUBLISHERS

If you are working with a fee-based publisher, be doubly aware of shoddy work, poor design and price gouging. I advise any serious writer to stay away from fee-based publishers. They may be all right for someone that wants a small collection of poems or their memoirs printed and bound for family or friends, but your local printer may do a better job for a lot less expense. Self-publishing through a ligament printer is not the same as fee-based publishing. If you are not sure of the differences between royalty-publishing, self-publishing and fee-based publishing you are not ready to self-publish.

CHECK LIST

- Proof and reproof your final cover for spelling and punctuation. It is amazing how many spelling errors appear on the covers, especially in titles and writers' names. It is so easy to miss the obvious.
- Check margins, trim, folds and spine alignment, and if applicable flaps, you don't want that important some-

thing cut off. Changes at press time are time consuming and expensive.

- If you supplied the bar code, take a proof-cover to a bookstore and have it scanned, to make sure is reads properly and is correct.
- Make sure there are no omissions or items left off. Sometime masks are not opened in the plating process, however that is unlikely with digital printing, it is usually human error. Sometime there are computer errors that appear after a file is converted or uploaded. Don't assume anything, reproof.
- If the cover sample is printed, check color and quality. It never gets better than the proof.

DON'T GIVE UP YOUR DREAMS

When my wife finished reading this manuscript, she said, "It really makes you think twice about self-publishing." I have given the reader a lot of information from years of experience, not only from the production end, but from the business end as well. And yes, I want you to think twice before you decide to enter the world of self-publishing. Self-publishing is challenging and there are charlatans that will pray on the unwary, but that could be said about any endeavor. Self-publishing can be fulfilling and greatly rewarding if you are willing to put in the effort. And a whole lot of fun. Take your time, learn the ropes, and develop your writing skills, design skills, your computer skills and marketing savvy. Go forward with your eyes wide open. Dream big dreams and never give them up. See you on the mountain someday soon.

Table of Illustrations

Resources

BOOKS

Aiming at Amazon: Aaron Shepard, Shepard Publications, Friday Harbor, WA

The Right Way to Write, Publish and Sell Your Book: Patricia Fry. Matilija Press, Ojai CA

The Chicago Manual of Style: University of Chicago Press, Chicago. IL.

Writer's Market: Writer's Digest Book, Cincinnati, OH

The Elements of Style: William Strunk Jr., Longman, New York, NY

ADDITIONAL READING

The Writer's Journey: Christopher Vogler Michael Wiese Productions, Studio City, CA

The Artist Way: Julia Cameron: G.P. Putnam's Sons. New York, NY

WEBSITES

Bowkers, source for ISBN – www.bowkers.com

Bar Code Graphic – www.barcode-us.com

U.S. Copyright Office – www.copyright.org

Dreamstime stock photos – wwwdreamstime.com

IStockphoto – www.istockpnoto.com

PRINT ON DEMAND SUPPLIERS

CreateSpace – www.createspace.com

Lighting Source – www.lightingsorce.com

WRITER'S INFORMATION AND ORGANIZATION WEBSITE

SPAWN, Small Publishers, Artist and Writer Network – www.spawn,org

Aaron Shepard's publishing site – www.newselfpublishing.com

Practical information on book design – www.thebookdesigner.com

Author Gene Stirm's website – www.genestirm.com

Way West Productions – www.waywestproductions.com

Glossary

Backbone – The backing of a book where the pages are joined to the cover.

Bio – A brief statement about the author, generally reflecting their credentials as to the subject of the book.

Case bound – A hardcover book.

Camera ready – Graphic art and pasted type ready for a process camera to make a negative.

Comb binding – A plastic binding used to bind flat sheets of paper with a cover.

Digital format – Type, art or photographs in a computer format and stored as a computer file.

Display type – A decorative typestyle used for headlines and titles.

Electronic submission – A manuscript or formatted book digitized to be sent over the Web or by electronic mail.

Format – The layout of a book in a specified form or style.

Genre – Refers to the general classifications of writing such as nonfiction, novel, poetry or romance.

ISBN – International Standard Book Number, identifies a particular book, publisher and edition. ISBN are distributed by R.R. Bowler in the U.S. and are required for books sold in the retail market.

Illustrations – Drawings or photographs used in printed material.

JPAG – File extension, graphics file compression format.

Kern and Kerning – The horizontal space between letters.

Leading – The space between lines of type.

Letterpress – The process of printing from an inked raised surface.

Line Art – Graphics and drawings produced with black ink lines.

Manuscript – A book in type or handwritten form, before it has been formatted, printed and bound.

Memoir – A personal history usually of a lesser time period than a autobiography.

Mechanicals – Art board of graphic and type pasted up and ready to be photographed and printed.

Model release – A simple document giving a photographer permission to use a person's picture

Offset Printing – A process where an inked image on a flat lithographic plate is transferred to a rubber blanket and the blanket transfers the ink image to the paper.

PDF file – A Portable Document Format used to transmit computer files.

Perfect binding – A binding process used to make paper-back book books where the pages are glued to the cover.

Photoshop – A photo editing software manufactured by Adobe Systems Incorporated.

POD – Print On Demand, a process where a digitized book can be produced one book at a time

Royalty publisher – Refers to a publisher that assumes the cost of production and distribution of a book and pays the author a percentage of each book sold as a royalty.

Saddle Stitch – A binding process where cover is stapled to the pages at the fold.

Self-Publish – Refers to an author that assumes the cost of producing and marketing of their own book.

Spiral Binding – A process of binding the pages of a book to a cover with a spiral wire.

Subsidy publishing – Publisher that the author shares in the publishers cost and control.

Testimonials – Refers to favorable comments about a book and sometimes printed on the back cover.

Thumbnails – Refers to small drawing or sketch of a design make before finished art.

Typeset – The process of keying or applying a typestyle to copy or a manuscript.

Typestyle – All the letters and number of a single type design family.

Vanity Press – A subset of self-publishing where an author pays the total cost to produce their book and the publisher has no interest in the success of the book. Some link POD suppliers to vanity publishers and in some cases it may be true, but POD suppliers are replacing short-run commercial printers as a supplier of quality books. Vanity publishers on the other hand pray on unwary authors eager to see their work published.

Index

Also by Gene Stirm

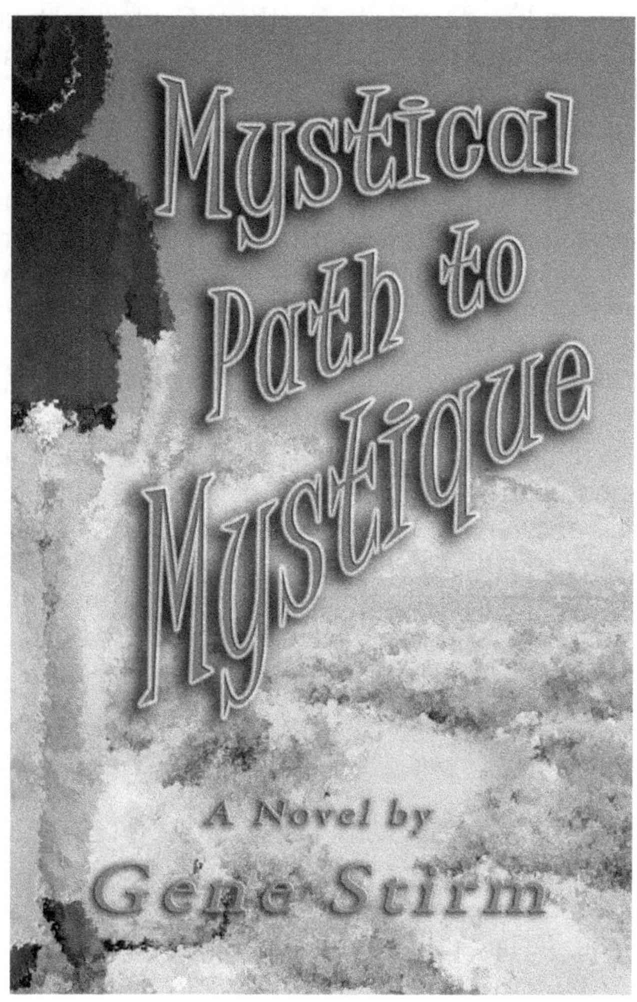

Mystical Path to Mystique by Gene Stirm

After a bump on the head, Dave, a crusty two timed divorced, ex LA ad man turned maintenance man, starts seeing a ghostly image of an American Indian, reflected in windows and mirrors. When he is fired from one more menial job on his long road to wreck and ruin, he makes a choice, get out of town. So he loads all his worldly possessions into the back of his pickup truck and heads to Northern California, to a piece of land he has inherited. On the way he picks up a mysterious hitchhiker, who takes him on the journey of a lifetime where all his hidden secrets are unmasked, and he is confronted by his past, his weaknesses and his fears. Can a simple act of forgiveness and letting go, actually bring happiness and fulfillment and could the beautiful widow he met at a rest stop be his sole mate, or is it all an illusion to snatch away just when he finds hope? Find out as you join Dave on his Mystical Path To Mystique.

Trent, the hitchhiker and half Native American, slowly reveals the fact that he is a Shaman and Mystic Traveler sent to help Dave find his way. However, when his own romantic involvement distract him, he must choose between personal passionate pleasure and a higher commitment in order to save Dave's life. And what of the ghostly Indian, is it a Spirit Guide sent to Dave or the effects of the bump on his head? This mystical romantic adventure makes many twists and turns on its way to Mystique.

Coming Soon by Gene Stirm

As A Shaman Dreams – Christmas 2010
A photographic book on California and Nevada Petroglyphs as seen through the eyes of a Shaman.

The Art and Craft of Book Design – Spring 2011
The companion book to The Art and Craft of Cover Design.

Scripted – Summer 2011
The epic journey of one man's life from before birth to after death.

www.ingramcontent.com/pod-product-compliance
Lightning Source LLC
LaVergne TN
LVHW020644100826
845148LV00012B/2333